This is a groundbreaking book. and insightful account it provi This account is inspiring and cl be awed by the work of the spirit in even the youngest

Bernadette Flanagan, SpIRE, Chairperson, Spirituality Institute for Research and Education, Dublin

This informative and engaging book sets out a strong case for the importance of meditation in the spiritual development of school-age children. Based on the personal voices of children engaged in school meditation, Dr Keating demonstrates the difference between the practical benefits of meditation and its deeper fruits of spiritual knowledge, greater clarity of perception, personal transformation, and authentic compassionate living. The study provides striking evidence of the depth of spiritual wisdom attained by school children through meditative practice.

Bernard McGinn, Naomi Shenstone Donnelley Professor Emeritus, Divinity School, University of Chicago

The research that Noel presents in his book provides clear evidence of the value of introducing the practice of meditation to primary school children. As the principal of a school where all the pupils participate in meditation twice a week, I recognise the benefits for the children's well-being and spiritual development that are described in this book. I am happy to endorse the book as a terrific resource for any principal or teacher who is interested in learning more about the nature of children's spirituality and how it can be nurtured through meditation.

Catriona O'Reilly, Principal, Our Lady of Good Counsel GNS, Ferrybank, Waterford

In this book Noel Keating gives us a magnificent and comprehensive explanation of how meditation enhances the lives of all, particularly children. With its extensive research and practical advice, this book is an invaluable tool for any teacher wishing to bring the benefits of meditation into his or her class. It holds pride of place in my classroom's Sacred Space, and I wholeheartedly recommend it.

Pauline Phelan, Fourth Class Teacher, St Joseph's GNS, Mountmellick, Co. Laois

In this highly accessible and well-informed book. Noel Keating takes us on an insightful journey into the little-known world of children's meditation. Further enriched by children's reflections on their experiences, the text offers much food for thought for student teachers and experienced teachers alike, illustrating how the practice has potential to nourish young people's spirituality.

Professor Kate Adams, Director of Research and Knowledge Exchange, University of Winchester

I am delighted to be associated with Noel Keating's work in promoting Christian Meditation with Children on a whole school basis. His research demonstrates that through this initiative many young people will appreciate more the wonder of their own being, their connectedness with humanity and all of creation, and the presence of the Holy Spirit at the deepest point of their existence. This book shows how children's lives can be transformed through meditation; society could be transformed if enough people participate.

Fr John McGarvey, PP Ballinasloe, Diocese of Clonfert

This book will be of immense value to teachers in understanding how the practice of meditation impacts positively on the spiritual development of children. The testaments of the children in the study bear witness to my own experience of teaching eight to twelve year olds to meditate for several years. The lessons presented are well constructed and easily adapted to suit the age and experience of a range of children in the primary school. I am sure that this book will inspire and give confidence to teachers who wish to introduce, promote and maintain the practice in the school setting in the years ahead.

Noreen Kelly, Teacher, St Francis Xavier NS, Dublin

During the last few years I have been spending a lot of my time with teachers who want to introduce the practice of Christian Meditation in their schools. I really welcome Noel Keating's authoritative guide to the ways that teachers can learn to do this; how they can learn from the children they teach and the rich range of resources that is identified to ensure the purity of the message and the sustainability of the practice. I'm happy to endorse his findings and also believe that this book will prove a worthy companion to 'Share the Gift', a six-week online course for teachers, which the World Community for Christian Meditation (WCCM) is currently introducing.

Charles Posnett, WCCM online courses coordinator for Meditation with Children, sharethegift@wccm.org

MEDITATION
WITH **CHILDREN**
A Resource for Teachers
and Parents

NOEL KEATING

VERITAS

Published 2017 by Veritas Publications
7–8 Lower Abbey Street
Dublin 1, Ireland
publications@veritas.ie
www.veritas.ie

ISBN 978 1 84730 800 9

10 9 8 7 6 5 4 3 2 1

Extract on page 86 from 'Having Confessed' by Patrick Kavanagh is reprinted from *Collected Poems*, edited by Antoinette Quinn (Allen Lane, 2004), by kind permission of the Trustees of the Estate of the late Katherine B. Kavanagh, through the Jonathan Williams Literary Agency.

Extract on page 200 from 'Hagia Sophia: Dawn' by Thomas Merton is reprinted from *In the Dark before Dawn: New Selected Poems of Thomas Merton*, Lynn R. Szabo (ed.), New York: New Directions, 2005.

Figure 1.3, p. 30 © Allan Ajifo
Figure 4.4, p. 135 © Elaine Keating

A catalogue record for this book is available from the British Library.

Cover designed by Heather Costello, Veritas Publications
Image concept inspired by Elaine Keating
Printed in the Republic of Ireland by SPRINT-print Ltd, Dublin

Veritas books are printed on paper made from the wood pulp of managed forests. For every tree felled, at least one tree is planted, thereby renewing natural resources.

Dedicated to Ella – a source of deep joy

Contents

List of Figures

Foreword

Nine-year-old Emilia sums it up when she describes how it feels when she meditates, saying, 'I feel joy but I am not just filled with joy, I am filled with happiness. I'm filled with calmness. I'm filled with everything. It feels like goodness is flowing through me.'

Having spent forty years of his professional life in the education of children, and having discovered the practice of meditation for himself, Noel Keating turned his attention to the spiritual life of the child. He was concerned about how the child as a whole was being educated among today's frenetic and compulsive concern with economic markets, league tables and scores. This book distils his experience and gives teachers and parents alike a groundbreaking interpretation of what he has discovered.

The distinction between meditation and mindfulness is of course essential to any faith-filled understanding of this topic. Over many years now, the successful mindfulness movement has opened a door in education – and many other social institutions – towards a deeper and richer understanding of the spiritual dimension of the human and of all forms of human activity. Mindfulness itself, avoiding any spiritual language or interpretation, did not go through the door it opened.

It is time now for us to go through that door and to promote a deeper and more integrated understanding. Meditation is

not just about relaxation or being aware of one's thoughts and sensations – valuable as this is in a stressed-filled life. It is – as Emilia experienced – about being deeply transformed and 'filled with everything'.

In this book, Noel Keating and the children to whom he has given a voice, present an exciting and urgent challenge to Christian leaders, to teachers and parents. Unusually for his own time, Jesus saw children as implicit teachers of their elders. 'Unless you become like little children, you will never enter the kingdom of heaven,' he said. As with many of Jesus' statements, this has been misunderstood by generations.

Becoming like a child does not mean becoming simplistic, passive or deferential. It means being open and participatory – at a later stage of development – to the ultimate mystery and meaning of existence. That children have this openness and can even, in their own limited but unforgettably enlightening way, give expression to it is now undeniable.

Professor Bernard McGinn, one of the world's foremost scholars of western mysticism, saw this, to his delight and surprise, when he heard Noel Keating reflect on his conversations with children about their experience of meditation. As he heard the comments children make about meditation, Professor McGinn remarked that they understood God and could give expression to their experience at least as well as the great mystics like John of the Cross, Julian of Norwich or Meister Eckhart.

What we learn from meditating with children offers us new paradigms for our troubled and lost times. The World Community for Christian Meditation is now teaching

10

meditation in schools in thirty countries. What Noel Keating has studied and researched with Irish children is a most timely and valuable contribution to the new whole-person, spiritual understanding of education that we should not hesitate any more to apply, for the benefit of the children in our care and for their children.

This book will help teachers to understand their vocation and make their task easier. They will learn from the child who said, 'I sometimes feel like it is sunrise when I am meditating and I feel like I'm not bored with school anymore'. Parents will be moved and find themselves challenged when they read seven-year-old Helena saying that when you meditate 'you feel like you are where you always wanted to be since you were small'.

For all these reasons this is an important, well-researched, intelligent and most welcome book for our time.

Laurence Freeman OSB

Acknowledgements

I wish to express my gratitude to the many people who have assisted in the preparation of this book. To Donna Doherty, Leeann Gallagher and the whole team at Veritas, I thank you for your encouragement and for challenging me along the way.

This book draws on my doctoral research and I would like to thank the principals, coordinators and teachers of the four schools that participated in my doctoral research for their full and thoughtful cooperation with the process. I was made to feel very welcome every time I visited and it was deeply inspiring to witness their commitment to the meaningful whole-school practice of meditation.

I want to say a special word of thanks to the seventy children who participated in the research for their openness and generosity of spirit. Their willingness to meet with me and to talk openly and deeply about their experience of the practice and its benefits and fruits in their lives is greatly appreciated. I was very often inspired by their words of wisdom and humbled by the simplicity and depth of their spirituality. I thank their parents for their permission to speak with their children.

I want to thank those who agreed to read the text as it was being completed, especially Pauline Phelan, Noreen Kelly and Fr John Garvey, and I am very appreciative of the written endorsements I received from them and others.

I would like to express my appreciation to Professor Michael Howlett (WIT) for his unfailing courtesy and his professional guidance over recent years as I undertook the research which informs this book. Thanks also to Dr Bernadette Flanagan, former Director of Research at All Hallows College, Dublin and current chairperson of SpIRE (the Spirituality Institute for Research and Education) who acted as a critical friend from time to time. I am grateful to her and to Dr Michael O'Sullivan, Director of SpIRE, for ensuring that the Masters in Spirituality programme grows from strength to strength and for helping me to understand research as a contemplative practice.

I owe a special debt of gratitude to my wife, Mary. Her incredible patience and encouragement and unfailing support in so many ways enabled me to devote time and energy to the research and to writing this book. I want to thank our daughter Elaine for her assistance with graphic design along the way and our sons Fergal and Brendan for their constant support.

My heart filled with joy at the birth of my grand-daughter Ella as my research was drawing to a close and I have watched her miraculous growth since then. May she grow in consciousness of her true-self and live her life from that deep awareness. I dedicate this book to her.

Introduction

This book explores the practice of meditation and its benefits and fruits for the individual and society. It distinguishes between the secular practice of mindfulness and meditation as a spiritual practice. At the heart of the book is an exploration of the child's experience of meditation: what it can be like for a child to meditate and how they say they experience its practical benefits and deeper inner fruits. It is a key aim of the book to give voice to the experience of children and to articulate especially, in their own words, how they experience its rich spiritual fruits in their lives. I hope this will encourage the practice of meditation with children in the home, and in the school and parish. And I hope to demonstrate how one can build on the popularity of mindfulness to generate a greater interest in the deeper fruits of meditation as, for example, in my own tradition of Christian meditation.

Meditation might be described as a practice which leads one beyond thoughts and feelings to a state of simple presence in which one is present to reality as it is in the moment. What exactly is meant by this will become clearer as the reader proceeds through the book.

In recent decades, mindfulness and meditation practices have gained widespread popularity. In particular, mindfulness has come to be widely accepted by health professionals as a very effective holistic intervention. This is due in no small measure to the work of Jon Kabat-Zinn, who developed and promoted the practice of Mindfulness-Based Stress Reduction (MBSR) and Mindfulness-Based Cognitive Therapy (MBCT) within the health sector, beginning in the 1970s. A great deal of research has been carried out over the last forty-five years that demonstrates the practical, pragmatic benefits of the practice and these will be outlined in chapter one. It is sufficient to say here that research confirms that mindfulness and meditation practices have significant physical, psychological, cognitive and emotional benefits for those who take the time to practise them regularly.

It is less widely known that meditation can also bear deeper fruit in the human person and, consequently, in society. While the wisdom traditions of the world have always asserted that meditation promotes human flourishing at a very deep spiritual level, very little research has been undertaken to explore its extent.[1] Part of the difficulty lies in defining what is meant by the terms I have just used. What is meant by 'spiritual'? What is 'human flourishing' and how can it be measured? Whereas one can physically measure changes in blood pressure, in levels of stress reduction and so on, how can one measure growth in a person's humanity or in their inner flourishing or their spiritual development?

This book seeks to explore some of these questions and describes how meditation can and does impact on the innate spirituality of the person, including children. I refer to this kind of impact – this growth in human flourishing at a deeper spiritual level – as the *fruits* of meditation. In other words, this book distinguishes between the practical, pragmatic, down-to-earth outcomes of meditation – describing them as benefits

– and the effects of the deeper, inner flourishing, which are described as fruits of the practice. While this book will serve as a very useful introduction to meditation for beginners, it is designed primarily for teachers and parents who may wish to introduce the practice of meditation to children.

This work is informed by three main sources. Firstly, it examines what the wisdom traditions and religions of the world have to say about the benefits and fruits of the practice. Secondly, it draws upon the work of the Meditation with Children project which has been running in many Irish primary schools in recent years.[2] And finally, this text draws on my doctoral research conducted between 2013 and 2017, which examines the child's experience of meditation in the context of such whole-school practice.

A central tenet of this book is that very real benefits and deep inner fruits flow from the practice of meditation; however, merely reading a book will not bring them about! The benefits and fruits flow from daily, or at least regular, meditation.[3] In some ways, the ideal book on meditation would be no longer than a paragraph, containing only a simple instruction on how to meditate. So, why have I written a book about it? I have done so to encourage and inspire you to take up, and persist with, the practice. But please understand that the benefits and fruits do not happen overnight. Sometimes others will see the change in you before you see it in yourself. I noticed the change when I realised that people were smiling at me more often than in the past! Of course, that probably happened because I was more relaxed and easy-going and I smiled at them first, but this was not an active choice. It had not sunk into my consciousness that meditation had changed my way of seeing and being in the world. I have written this book so that you can know how powerful the practice is – not just on the surface of your life but at a very deep, personal level. Ultimately, at the level of meaning and identity, as you begin to discover who you really are at the very depth of your being.

If you intend to help others to take up the practice, especially if you intend to introduce children and young people to meditation, for that to be fully authentic it will help if you have personal experience of it and if you genuinely understand the core message – that meditation leads to deep inner and outer flourishing. Of course, you can teach it and explain that those who practise it have experienced the benefits and fruits, but it helps enormously if that truth is manifest in who you are, if meditation has helped you to see the world differently and helped change your relationship and encounter with it. I have included a brief exercise at the end of each chapter and I invite and encourage you to take those opportunities to practise meditation for yourself.

The book begins by exploring the origins of mindfulness and meditation practices in the different wisdom and religious traditions of the world and how they differ in their core intention; it locates the practice of Christian meditation within this and describes Christian meditation in a language accessible in a secular society (chapter one). Chapter one also explores the practical benefits of meditation and what children have to say about their experience of those benefits. The first practical exercise (interlude) follows. It explores how to meditate and gives the reader an opportunity to get a sense for themselves of what is involved in the practice. Chapter two outlines what the religious traditions describe as the spiritual fruits of meditation. Chapter three explores the topic of meditation with children and gives an account of what children themselves have to say about their personal experience of meditation, while chapter four describes what children have to say about their experience of its deep inner fruits in their lives. This is followed, in chapter five, by a set of three practical lessons that may be used to introduce children to the practice of meditation. Chapter six contains two further lessons on how to speak with children about the deeper fruits of meditation. The book concludes in chapter five with a brief summary of the key points. The reader may choose their own path through the material.

Endnotes

1. Wisdom traditions are typically found in the religions of the world, especially in the contemplative traditions of Buddhism, Christianity, Vedanta, Daoism, Sufism, and in the history of philosophy. Most of the wisdom traditions evolved during the Axial Age, between 900 and 200 BCE. Karen Armstrong suggests that in this period of history, people worked as hard to find a cure for their spiritual ills as we do today trying to find a cure for cancer. They were not interested in belief or doctrine but in discovering a way that transformed the individual for the better and for the good of society.

2. This project was started in 2012 with a view to inviting Irish primary schools to take up the practice of meditation (based on the Christian tradition) on a whole-school basis. At the time of writing, the project was active in one hundred and fifty primary schools across Ireland, with about thirty-five thousand children engaging in the whole-school practice of meditation several times each week. The project is supported by Christian Meditation Ireland, which offers free training to schools. More information available on: www.christianmeditation.ie.

3. As Jon Kabat-Zinn observes, 'The very intention to practise with consistency and gentleness – whether you feel like it or not on any given day – is a powerful and healing discipline.' Jon Kabat-Zinn, *Mindfulness for Beginners: Reclaiming the Present Moment – and Your Life*, Boulder, CO: Sounds True, 2012, p. 2.

Chapter One

The Origins and Benefits of Meditation

Meditation as a Secular, Holistic Practice

Meditation was popularised in the West in the 1960s with the spread of transcendental meditation.[1] Starting in the 1970s, meditation was developed as the holistic practice of mindfulness for the reduction of stress at the University of Massachusetts by Jon Kabat-Zinn.[2] In the intervening years, it gained widespread acceptance in the field of holistic medicine and is recognised in general medical practice as a beneficial intervention. Modern society has come to acknowledge that mindfulness is an effective means of achieving a better balance in life. It acknowledges that in an increasingly busy and frantic world we all need a break from external noise and stress. Think of how stressful and noisy modern life is: we spend our time moving from one urgent task to the next, from one sensational piece of news to the next, from one commitment to the next. We are inundated with stimuli from the moment we wake until we fall sleep, exhausted, at the end of the day. Our minds are busy all the time. Even in our 'time out', technology and social media intrude incessantly. There is an urgent need for silence and stillness in the modern world and meditation practice makes that possible.

Meditation with Children

Children see how adults behave and they become conditioned to think that this is how life must be. Much that children experience today inhibits their innate understanding of the need for stillness and silence. They too are bombarded from an early age with all kinds of noise and stimuli. Even when they are alone, they keep themselves busy on tablets and smartphones. In today's world many children live demanding, stressful lives. Meditation helps to counter this, creating an opportunity for quiet recollection in their lives.[3] There are many things we can do to give ourselves a break from such unrelenting pressure, such as changing our patterns, going for long walks or going out into nature away from the demands of a busy life. These are all useful. Meditation is an alternative, additional strategy that we can access at anytime and anywhere. It costs nothing and, when practised on a whole-school basis, it can bring benefits and fruits not just for each child and teacher but also for the school as a community.

Because I spend a lot of my working hours at a computer, I sometimes suffer from stiffness in my neck and shoulders and I need to seek out physiotherapy to resolve the issue. It releases tension and restores harmony in our bodies. As well as massaging the muscles, my physiotherapist applies pressure to what she calls 'trigger points'. These are points at which nerve endings connect to muscle fibres and where overload can cause the muscle to spasm. Applying pressure firmly to these trigger points blocks the signals from the nerve endings and the muscles cease to spasm. The absence of 'noise' allows the restoration of muscles to their normal, relaxed state. Meditation does the same for the human psyche. Silence is like a circuit breaker – it breaks the incessant pattern of unrelenting stimuli and noise. It reduces both internal and external 'noise' and stress and restores us to harmony.

Meditation as a Spiritual Practice

Although the practice of meditation has gained enormously in popularity in the last fifty years, it has been around for thousands of years and can be found in almost all of the wisdom traditions and religions of the world. It seems that from long before recorded time, the Aboriginal people of Australia practised a form of deep inner listening and waiting called *dadirri*. The earliest written records on meditation come from the Hindu traditions of Vedantism in ancient India and go back approximately three and a half thousand years to around 1500 BCE.[4] Their ancient scriptures, the *Upanishads* and the *Bhagavad Gita*, place the exercise of stillness and non-judgemental attention at the centre of human growth and well-being.[5] The first written records of Buddhist meditation go back to the first century BCE, but the practice appears to date to at least several centuries before then.[6] Buddhism developed in China, as Zen, where it was influenced by Taoism. Judaism has its own contemplative tradition while the practice of meditation in the Christian tradition can be traced to the Desert Fathers and Mothers at the end of the third century CE. Islam too has a contemplative tradition, called Sufism.

Some who write about Celtic spirituality refer to the practice of *anal-duccaid* as a form of 'breath prayer', and the Irish word for contemplation is *rinnfheitheamh*, which literally translates as 'waiting at the edge', suggesting that the practice may have been known and practised in pre-Christian Celtic cultures also.

Meditation, then, is an ancient practice and there are many variations of it. To be fully understood, each one must be considered within its own context. That context includes the intention behind the practice; in other words, what each tradition sees as the purpose of meditation. But it is a common understanding of the wisdom and religious traditions that meditation promotes greater self-awareness, individual and communal well-being and human flourishing.[7]

Kinds of Meditation

The word meditation carries different meanings in different contexts. For the purposes of this text, however, it refers to practices that involve intentional silence and stillness. For many, it is practised with a view to achieving a state of consciousness that might be described as 'pure awareness' or 'object-less awareness', a state of pure presence beyond all thoughts and feelings. It is a state of alert relaxation in which one is aware of, but not caught up in or captivated by, our thoughts and emotions. As well as promoting the development of clarity and concentration, many traditions of meditation hold that it enables the practitioner to perceive objectively the true nature of present-moment reality.

Meditation practices can be said, by and large, to fall into two main categories: focused-attention meditation and open-monitoring meditation. Focused-attention meditation generally involves a process of sitting in silence, with the aim of being still in body and mind. This stillness is brought about through the narrowing of focus to the object of meditation, which may be a word, a phrase, the physical sensation of the breath or even an object of some kind. Whenever the practitioner becomes aware that their attention has wandered and they realise they are caught up in their thoughts or emotions, the meditator gently but firmly brings their attention back to the meditation object. In Eastern traditions, this is usually the breath, while Western traditions often favour a word or mantra. It is a common understanding across the traditions of focused-attention meditation that human experience is mediated by the bodily senses and interpreted by the mind, which seeks to make sense and meaning of experience. They also agree that meditation heightens awareness of the experience of the present moment as the focused attention helps to quieten the self-conscious mind. While the practice remains much the same in focused-attention meditation across different traditions, the intention may vary. Intention plays an important role in meditation and may impact on outcomes. The kind of meditation addressed in this book is focused-attention meditation.

The second variety of meditation, open-monitoring meditation, is the kind practised in mindfulness. It involves paying attention to whatever comes into awareness; it may be a thought, emotion, or bodily sensation. Practitioners are advised to simply become conscious of whatever is currently in awareness and to follow it until something else emerges – but without trying to hold onto it or change the content of awareness in any way. Jon Kabat-Zinn, for example, defines the practice of mindfulness meditation as 'paying attention ...

on purpose, in the present moment, and non-judgementally'.[8] To be mindful is to be aware of what is happening in the present moment. Focused-attention meditation cultivates mindfulness and promotes greater self-awareness, as we shall see. Likewise, mindfulness practices – such as paying attention to the body, to ambient sounds, to inner thoughts and emotions, eating mindfully – can be an excellent preparation for silent, focused-attention meditation.

It is common practice across the diverse traditions of meditation to recommend that adults meditate twice each day for a period of twenty to thirty minutes each time. As a rule of thumb, children are encouraged to meditate for one minute per year of their age, ideally every day.[9]

Practical Benefits of Meditation

Shanida Nataraja has written a scientific guide to meditation and the brain that explores such research in considerable detail and concludes that practices such as meditation impact positively on measurable health outcomes. There is a growing body of evidence, especially since the turn of the millennium, that 'points towards the benefit of regular meditation and the role that it plays in enhancing human performance and maintaining good health and well-being'.[10] Research on adults and children has shown the pragmatic benefits of meditation and mindfulness practices on reducing distress, enhancing general well-being and impacting positively on basic brain function and habits of the mind. In brief, meditation gives rise to a sense of calm, peace and balance that benefits both overall health and emotional well-being. These benefits arise whether meditation is practised from a secular or spiritual perspective.[11] As we shall see in the next chapter, however, the practice is even more powerful when it operates within the context of 'a person's deepest religious or philosophical convictions'.[12]

The practical, pragmatic benefits of meditation identified by such scientific research – for adults and children – can be summarised under four key headings, as indicated in Figure 1.1. In other words, meditation benefits physical and mental health, enhances emotional well-being and improves cognitive function.[13]

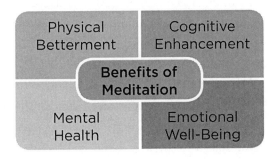

Figure 1.1 Practical Benefits of Meditation

The positive effects on *physical health* include reduced blood pressure, a positive impact on cholesterol levels, reduced cortisol (the stress hormone) levels, hence reduced anxiety and stress, improved immune function, improved skin clearing in psoriasis and symptom relief in irritable bowel syndrome, improved glycaemic control in diabetes, improved symptoms in heart disease, symptom control in patients with fibromyalgia.

Meditation seems to help mental health by optimising brain function. It leads to improved decision-making, improvements in problem-solving skills, better coping strategies, a more positive attitude towards perceived stress, and a decreased tendency to self-reference. Studies suggest that it can also reduce the risk of relapse or recurrence in depression, and can reduce risk-prone behaviour.

Meditation leads to a heightened sense of emotional well-being, enhanced openness, and improved self-esteem. It leads to greater emotional stability, to a decrease in stress and anxiety, and to a reduction in negative emotions and worrying. One becomes more openly curious and receptive to new experiences. As one's emotional intelligence expands, the practice can also lead to improved social function and a greater capacity for enjoying life.

Meditation also enhances cognitive function. The positive effects include the cultivation of a more observing attitude, improved attention, a greater focus on the present moment, increased sustained attention, better reasoning and creativity and insightful problem-solving. One becomes less prone to distractions; distractions still arise but one develops a capacity not to be drawn into them and to remain focused on the task at hand.

How Children Describe the Practical Benefits of Meditation

In my research, I spoke with seventy children from four schools participating in the Meditation with Children project. The purpose was to allow the children to describe what meditation was like for them and to assess if they experienced any benefits and/or fruits as a result of it. I interviewed each child twice, about three weeks apart.

- ~ Helps You Let Go of All the Drama
- ~ Calms & Restores You
- ~ Generates Energy & Confidence
- ~ Helps You Make Better Decisions

Benefits

Figure 1.2 How Children Describe the Benefits of Meditation

Overall, the children's experience confirmed the positive findings of previous international research among adults. As we shall see below, the children found that meditation: (i) enables them to let go of all the drama; (ii) calms and relaxes them and restores them to a sense of well-being; (iii) generates energy and confidence in them; (iv) improves their capacity for decision-making. For each benefit, I give some examples of how the children gave expression to it. While some children referred to physical betterment, a key benefit identified by the adult research, it did not emerge as a common theme with the children as a whole.

Meditation Helps You 'Let Go of All the Drama'

This description is taken from Leanne (9), who said that when meditating in school, 'It feels like we can have a break from all the drama and leave it behind us.' Frank (9) expressed it in his own way, saying, 'I like the way it just gets all your thoughts out of your mind and it relaxes you so you're not always thinking about "bothering" stuff. You can relax and all of your worries go away.' Frank had recently begun to meditate on Friday mornings before he left for school because he worries about his spelling tests.

Sarah (9) mentioned that she often meditated before an important football match, 'As soon as I am dressed for the game, I take some time out [to meditate] so I won't be worried about the game'. Others did likewise for swimming, basketball and dancing competitions. Barry (10) mentioned

Figure 1.3 Left and Right Brain Hemispheres

that, when playing basketball, he meditates briefly before taking a free throw, 'because I usually tense up in a basketball match when I'm taking a free throw. So, I meditate for about ten seconds before I take the shot'. During the interviews, children identified some images which reminded them of meditation. Many children chose an image depicting the two hemispheres of the brain (Figure 1.3). The children pointed to the colourful right hemisphere to indicate how meditation made them feel – happy and relaxed.

Lucy (10) said that the thing she really liked about meditation was that she didn't have to use her brain to figure things out like she did in maths class. She wasn't sure what part of her was working when she meditated but she thought it might be her heart, because, 'Your heart tells you what you really like, and I really like meditation.' Barry (10) said that meditation feels 'like my whole body is shutting down'. His mind clears, 'It feels like words are just going away and the only word I have left is "Maranatha".'

Meditation Calms and Restores You

Almost all of the children in the study claimed that meditation calmed and relaxed them. It was far and away the most common answer to the prompts, 'What do you like about meditation?' and 'Why do people meditate?' Derek (9) said he liked meditation because, 'It makes me feel relaxed and it makes me feel calm and it stops me thinking about bad things'. Emelia (9) said, 'A good thing about meditation is that you can do it all the time and you can just feel relaxed and not be angry, or sad, or worried about something. You can just meditate'. When Emelia talked about meditation she used the word 'joy' very often – 'I feel joy but I am not just filled with joy, I'm filled with happiness, I'm filled with calmness, I'm filled with everything.' – suggesting that when she let go of her worries, joy and peace and happiness came up to the surface. Kate (11) felt that after meditation she has a sense that 'everything is going right even if it feels like it's going wrong'.

Natalie (11) said, 'Meditation helps me to handle pain better'. Referring to the recent death of her grandad, she explained, 'I meditated every day and it really helped me. It made me realise that he had been going through pain every day and I was happy he wasn't in pain any more. So, even though I missed him, I was able to let him go.' Without exception, the children found that meditation cleared their minds of worries and anxieties, relaxing them and restoring them to a state of peacefulness and calmness.

Meditation Gives You Energy and Confidence

Children felt more energetic, more focused and more confident when regularly practising meditation. For example, Norah (10) observed, 'Every time I do meditation, I feel I'm more bouncy. I have energy inside me and I just feel like I'm really happy'. Leanne (9) noted, 'Meditation makes me feel joyful because it gives me more energy. And I can deal with things that annoy me. If my brother is just being annoying, I can let it bounce off my chest and ignore it'. She also found meditation gave her confidence, saying:

> Before I started meditating I was very shy and was often scared to say what I wanted to say. But now I think that my confidence has grown and I'm opening up my heart for the words that are just locked in there, I'm able to say them now ... It makes me feel that I can do anything if I put my mind to it. It makes me think of the saying 'Nothing is impossible' when I meditate because it just feels like I can do anything.

Grace (9) mentioned:

> I sometimes feel like it's the sunrise when I'm meditating, because I'm feeling more awake and I'm feeling like I'm not bored any more in school. I feel like I'll put up my hand more in class. I take part more as well.

Rowan (9) said that if her school stopped meditating, 'It would make me very angry because I need that meditation. It makes me feel more relaxed and more confident to ask questions in class, more than I usually do.' Derek (9) commented that sometimes other boys will taunt him about his ability to do something, 'They pretty much dissolve my confidence and stop me from doing it. But when I meditate the confidence rises up inside of me and it helps me. And I go and do it.'

Rowan (9) was one of many children who found meditation helped with their homework:

> Sometimes I get stuck on my homework and I know now that if I just meditate for a bit it will help. It helps me to concentrate and I'm more relaxed to do my homework. And I realise that it's alright to be stuck because you learn from that. It's okay to make mistakes, because you learn from your mistakes.

Commonly children reported that meditation energised them, helped them focus on tasks, and made them more confident, better able to tackle challenges, test themselves in unfamiliar situations and seize new opportunities. It also gave rise to greater creativity and improved problem-solving ability.

Meditation Helps You to Make Better Decisions

Many of the children observed that meditation helped them to think more clearly and make better choices. This usually had to do with developing the capacity to stand back from a challenging situation, to be deliberately thoughtful about it and to respond appropriately rather than react out of upset or anger. Rowan (9) describes how she handles it now when her brother or her family annoy her, 'I ask myself if they are doing it to annoy me. Meditation helps me to figure it out because it relaxes me. It gives me more confidence and it makes me smarter.' In other words, meditation taught Rowan to not react immediately, but instead to take a moment and think before responding. Helena (7) found that meditation helped her to be more thoughtful, thinking before acting:

> Sometimes when I'm really, really mad and angry, I feel like I want to say something mean to someone. But now I think before I act because when I meditate it makes me think before I react.

Antoni (11) observed, 'I can see deeper into things, not just see what they are on the surface. So, you can talk to people and not just argue with them.' Frank (9) picked up on the metaphor of a muddy window, used to explain the benefits of meditation, saying, 'If you are angry about something, the window will be all muddied but when you are calm, you get a clear picture.'

Derek (9) commented that meditation helps him to accept things and do the right thing:

> Meditation makes me feel open-minded. Whenever I have something bad happening in my life, I usually don't want to think about it, so I try to forget it. But when I meditate I find I do think about it and then I do the right thing. A little while ago I was being bullied. I was upset and didn't want anyone to know. But then I took meditation and I thought about it afterwards. I didn't refuse it. I told my mom what had happened.

Lena (11) felt that meditation had changed her for the better, because it helps her to solve problems and frees her to do the right thing:

> When you do meditation it mostly relaxes you and you figure out what not to do and what to do. When you meditate, you are more independent than you have been before you meditated. So, when forgotten memories rush back and all of these things go through your mind, you are able to say, 'You know what, that's all in the past, let that go. You are more independent now.'
>
> You are able to work things out. Some people think that shouting and screaming at the other person is the way to handle things – but actually it's not. It's better to calm down, to explain what you feel and to sort things out that way.

Regularly, children credited meditation with improving their decision-making skills and enhancing their capacity to stand back and reflect thoughtfully on a problem. In particular, they developed a capacity to look at problems more objectively, to adopt a changed perspective that highlights their own contribution to a problem as well as the factors that may have motivated others to behave badly towards them.

How Do These Benefits Flow from Meditation?

Shanida Nataraja suggests that these benefits arise because meditation heightens our awareness of habitual patterns and promotes whole-brain integration. In order to survive in the world, much of our repetitive behaviour takes place automatically; think how easy it becomes to drive a car or ride a bike after some practice but how difficult it is in the beginning when it is an entirely new activity. Just as putty records the imprint of a key, the brain records an imprint of experiences.[14] For optimal performance, our brain makes use of this imprinted experience by making actions automatic, rather than working through every detailed movement every time. There is a downside to this automation: we can easily become trapped by the automatic response, prisoners of our unconscious conditioning. Most of us remain unaware of how such unconscious conditioning governs our decisions and our reactions to events in life. There are so many ingrained habits that we take for granted and never question because we simply 'picked up' these standard ways of doing things – of reacting to life – from our family, our culture, and our society. Practising meditation on a regular basis increases our awareness of this conditioning and that awareness helps us to change.

The left and right hemispheres of the forebrain have quite different functions. Generally speaking, the left hemisphere is associated with analytical, rational and logical processing; it divides, reduces, fragments, analyses and is the seat of language. By contrast, the right hemisphere is associated with abstract thought, non-verbal awareness, intuition and holistic thought, visual-spatial perception, and the expression and modulation of emotions. Western culture has overstressed left-brain activity and most people in the West live out their daily lives in a way that is dominated by left-brain activity. Because of this imbalance, many people in Western society often fail to keep in touch with and honour feelings and emotions. Meditation helps to correct this imbalance, leading to greater integration of the two hemispheres of the brain as it interprets and responds to pre-reflective experience. Entering a meditative state calms the incessant chatter in our left hemisphere and moves our consciousness towards the right hemisphere. The regular practice of meditation helps to open neural pathways, bridges between the two hemispheres, giving rise to a more integrated way of being in the moment, a more cohesive mode of perceiving and thinking, which leads to a more balanced way of seeing and being in the world.

Can Meditation Have Adverse Effects?
Meditation is not a panacea for all the ills of the world but it clearly improves the quality of life for many people across a range of areas and functions. It will not alleviate every condition, every dis-ease, for every person; however, the evidence is clear that it brings significant benefits to those who meditate regularly. Nonetheless, it is sensible to ask whether there are circumstances where meditation can result in potential unpleasant or adverse side effects.

It is important to understand that emotions from traumatic life experiences may sometimes become buried deep in the unconscious and it is possible that during prolonged periods of meditation such emotions may rise to consciousness causing the practitioner to experience sadness or anger.[15] Martin Laird observes that 'very occasionally you hear of meditation bringing up certain underlying difficulties that are already present but not acknowledged. This is part of the healing nature of a serious contemplative discipline,' adding that 'the desert tradition [of Christianity] really did not speak of any harmful effects'.[16] Should that happen, a person is advised to discuss the matter with their doctor or counsellor but it should be stressed that the likelihood of it happening is very slim and linked to long rather than short periods of meditation. In any case, such an experience might prove to be ultimately beneficial, presenting an opportunity for personal growth through counselling. Caution is advised, especially regarding long meditation periods, when a participant suffers from post-traumatic stress disorder or psychosis.

In terms of physical health, there are some considerations for meditators who suffer from epilepsy to cater for the possibility that they may experience an episode during a meditation session, but that is not to suggest that meditation should be avoided. Regarding spiritual health, it is important to listen to and engage with anyone who may have religious concerns about the practice, and to encourage them to explore what their own religion has to say about it.

In respect of studies on mindfulness with children and adolescents, 'The consensus is that interventions are generally acceptable and well-liked by the participants, and there have been no reports that any of them caused harm (so called "adverse effects").'[17] No negative effects have been reported by any school participating in the Meditation with Children project.

Meditation Traditions Differ in their Intention

One can readily distinguish between secular mindfulness, the non-theistic wisdom traditions of the world, and the theistic traditions, which, like Christianity, see the human person as created by and invited to participate in a personal relationship with the divine. Meditation as a secular practice is understood as a technique for quieting the mind. But the wisdom traditions and religions of the world see it differently. They see it not as a way of making the mind quiet, but as a means of entering into the quiet that is already there. As Laurence Freeman expresses it, 'From a spiritual perspective you relax in order to meditate rather than meditating just in order to relax.'[18] This distinction highlights the intention of the meditator as an important factor in meditation. I suggest that one can identify three broad forms of intention in meditation: meditation practised from a secular perspective, meditation practised from a spiritual but non-theistic spiritual or religious perspective, and meditation practised from a theistic spiritual or religious perspective.

In secular meditation – as, for example, in Mindfulness-Based Stress Reduction (MBSR) – the intention primarily concerns the well-being of the meditator.[19] In that sense, the secular practice of meditation might be described as person-centred, focused on the well-being of the individual, in its initial intention.[20] Of course, while it may begin as an act of gentle kindness toward ourselves, having the benefit that we feel better about ourselves, by freeing us from our preoccupations, however temporarily, it can also lead us in the direction of loving kindness towards others. In faith-based, non-theistic meditation, the intention may be described as other-centred because it seeks not just the well-being of the practitioner but also the well-being of all humankind. For example, from a Buddhist perspective, mindfulness is about being in the present moment, looking deeply at reality, so that one can see clearly what is. Only from this perspective can a person act in true freedom. From the Buddhist viewpoint, meditation is a bridge that clarifies the connection between one's state of mindfulness and how one behaves in the world, between one's inner peace and peace on earth. As one begins to see the world as it really is, one 'can relate to it with compassion, kindness and wisdom'.[21] And, finally, in faith-based theistic traditions, such as Hinduism and Christianity, the intention may be described as Other-centred, with a capital 'O', meaning that the practice is centred on a divine being rather than the human ego, on discovering one's true essence in relation to the divine. In the Christian tradition, this Other is named as Christ. The Christian tradition teaches that one of the deep fruits of Christian contemplative practice is that it leads to a more authentic, more compassionate, Christ-centred way of being in the world. Christian meditation seeks the harmonious integration of body, mind and spirit.

In other words, in terms of initial intention, the tradition of secular meditation is centred on the self, the tradition of non-theistic faith-based meditation is other-centred and the tradition of theistic faith-based meditation is Other-centred.[22]

What makes Christian meditation distinctive is that it is Christ-centred and recognises the deep connectivity between the human spirit and the Holy Spirit. This is exemplified in the Christian tradition by the words of Psalm 46:10, 'Be still, and know that I am God.'

The Christian Tradition of Meditation

Intention is mysteriously but deeply impactful.[23] The Christian tradition holds that the practice of meditation as a daily discipline deepens one's appreciation of the divine spark deep within, nourishes one's inner life and, as a result, leads the practitioner to live life more abundantly and compassionately: 'The discipline of meditation ... places that one demand on us absolutely: that we must leave self behind so completely, leave our thoughts, our analyses, our feelings behind so completely, as to be totally at the disposition of the Other.'[24] While intention is important and impactful, it must also be effortless. Christian meditation is not about doing or achieving, but simply about being. Although effortless, it is not passive, but dynamic. The underlying dynamic is receptive and participative. It is not about mastery but mystery; not about mastering a technique but allowing oneself to be vulnerable to the mystery in which we live and move and have our being.[25]

In Christian meditation, one holds fast to the intention to be in communion with God in the silence but one lets go of all effort to make it happen. Christians believe that meditation opens us to the deep engagement between the human spirit and the divine at a level of consciousness deeper than our ordinary everyday awareness. Indeed, meditation 'is a eucharistic act because, like the Eucharist, it reveals and celebrates the real presence'.[26] As James Finley describes it, in the practice of meditation:

we freely choose to offer the least resistance to a graced liberation from the tyranny of thought. As we do so we open ourselves to the mystery of knowing God in ways that utterly transcend what thought can grasp or contain.[27]

It is because of this deep unconscious connection that the repeated regular practice of meditation results in rich spiritual fruits, leading the practitioner to an awareness of their true essence, their true-self.[28] Christians see all human persons as 'children of God' who have the innate capacity to be open to and live out of that awareness.[29]

Christian meditation is a very rich form of prayer. The *Catechism of the Catholic Church* speaks of three major expressions of prayer: vocal, meditative and contemplative (2699). There can be some confusion in modern terminology between the words 'meditation' and 'contemplation'. In the Christian tradition, the word 'meditation' has been used, as it is in the catechism, to denote discursive, mental reflection on a text; in other words, thinking about the meaning of a text and its implications for the life of the reader. By contrast, the word 'contemplation' traditionally refers to non-discursive, silent prayer – what the catechism calls 'a gaze of faith' (2715) and 'silent love' (2717).[30] Although John Main, the Benedictine monk who recovered and reimagined the practice of contemplation as followed by the Desert Fathers, ignored this distinction and named it 'Christian meditation', it is actually the practice of contemplation, a silent form of being-as-prayer.[31]

The *Catechism of the Catholic Church* defines prayer as 'the raising of one's mind and heart to God' (2590) and for very many laypeople, this has meant primarily listening to and reflecting on the word of God in Scripture and the activity of 'saying' one's prayers – all of which is very much a mental activity. Within the Christian tradition such discursive and imaginative forms of prayer are rightly regarded as very important; however, they came to be seen by many as the only way of prayer. By contrast, Christian meditation is a silent, wordless, imageless form of prayer that calls for stillness of body and mind. This tradition recognises that, as St John of the Cross expressed it, 'Silence is God's first language' and that silence is the deepest response to mystery. It might be said that the aim in Christian meditation is to make silence the language of our subjectivity.

According to the Christian faith, we are not only created by God and loved by God but, as our human spirit is transformed by the Holy Spirit, we also participate in God's own life and are destined for union in and with God (Jn 17:21). When we are present to our own spirit, our true-self, we are simultaneously present to God. Within the Christian tradition meditation is considered to be a very pure form of prayer. Indeed, for John Main the central task of the Christian life is to come into union, into communion and he saw meditation as *oratia pura*, pure prayer, a prayer of being in communion.[32] This form of prayer is understood more as something that happens to you, as the Spirit intercedes for you, than something you do (Rm 8:26). All you know is that you are being prayed and guided in the direction of your true-self; your intuitive understanding grows that it's not all about you and you become less wilful and more willing.

Prayer without words is not a recent phenomenon and is firmly rooted in the traditions of the early Church; however, for many people in the Western world today, engaging with silence is akin to speaking in a foreign language. The two approaches to Christian prayer described here as discursive and non-discursive are generally referred to as the 'kataphatic' tradition (prayer through words and images, discursive, conceptual) and the 'apophatic' tradition (prayer without images or words, non-discursive, contemplative). While the kataphatic tradition honours conceptual knowledge, the apophatic tradition honours the validity of perceptual, spiritual knowledge.[33] It is comfortable with the understanding that not all knowledge can be given full expression in words; indeed, it declares that some forms of truth are accessible and expressible only through silence and symbols. It recognises that remaining humbly open to mystery is vital for the integration of the mind and the heart. Christian meditation is often referred to as the prayer of the heart, because it places the focus on opening the heart to the Spirit. Just as the physical heart is the lifeblood of the body, the metaphorical heart is seen as the vital centre of our spiritual lives;[34] this is the heart referred to in St Augustine's well known phrase 'Our hearts are restless until they rest in Thee'.[35] Bernadette Flanagan notes that up until the seventeenth century 'mind and heart, were seen – not as conflicting – but rather as complementary ways of making meaning of the world'.[36] This understanding is being recovered slowly in the modern world through the practice of meditation, one of the fruits of which is an integration of conceptual and perceptual knowing. Meditation leads to wholeness which is, ultimately, true holiness.

Christian meditation has firm foundations in the teaching of Jesus and has a rich tradition in the Church, East and West.[37] In his teaching, Jesus was concerned with helping people become aware of the presence of God at the centre of their lives and he promoted the practice of silent, interior prayer:

> And when you pray, go into your private room, shut yourself in, and so pray to your Father who is in that secret place, and your Father who sees all that is done in secret will reward you. In your prayers do not babble like the gentiles do, for they think that by using many words they will make themselves heard. (Mt 6:5–7)

In the Christian tradition, meditation is a form of prayer in which one is not seeking for anything because 'your Father knows what you need before you ask him' (Mt 6:8). It is about opening one's heart to the Spirit within and allowing oneself to be nourished by love, allowing love to gaze at one as one sits in silence.

Jesus also taught by direct example – the Gospels recount many occasions when he 'withdrew himself into the wilderness, and prayed' (Lk 5:16). While it is clear that Jesus placed prayer at the centre of his life, one cannot be certain how he prayed.[38] But, from the many references to his practice of solitude and his sayings, such as 'I and the Father are One', it seems reasonable to suggest that his personal prayer may have been one of silent communion rather than words. The core elements of Jesus' teaching on prayer – interiority, silence, calmness, mindfulness and being in the present moment – are also the core elements of the practice of Christian meditation.[39]

In Christian meditation, the intention is to simply be in the presence of the divine within;[40] this presence is named as the Holy Spirit, which is conceived as the relationship of love that flows between the Father and the Son.[41] The following extract from St Paul's Letter to the Ephesians captures poetically the intention in Christian meditation:

> With this in mind, then, I kneel in prayer to the Father from whom every family in heaven and on earth takes its name, that out of the treasures of his glory he may grant you strength and power through his Spirit in your inner self, so that Christ may dwell in your hearts through faith. And then, planted in love and built on love, with all God's people you will have the strength to grasp the breadth and length, the height and depth, so that knowing the love of Christ, which is beyond knowledge, you may be filled with the utter fullness of God. (Eph 3:14–19)

Meditation, then, is about letting go of the ego and trusting in God – about inexpressible communion with God in the silence.[42] In other words, from the Christian perspective, the intention of silent meditation is to let go of the trivial to acknowledge and access that which is essential for the fullness of life.[43] It is simply about being with God. From a

Christian childlike perspective, about being with Jesus. In the words of John Main:

> The all-important aim in Christian meditation is to allow God's mysterious and silent presence within us to become more and more not only a reality, but the reality in our lives; to let it become that reality which gives meaning, shape and purpose to everything we do, to everything we are.[44]

Although the practice receded in the Western Church,[45] it resurfaced often through the centuries as witnessed, for example, by mystics such as Meister Eckhart (late thirteenth, early fourteenth century), Catherine of Siena and the anonymous author of *The Cloud of Unknowing* (fourteenth century), Julian of Norwich (late fourteenth, early fifteenth century) and St Teresa of Ávila (sixteenth century). The theme of *The Cloud of Unknowing* is that God cannot be reached by the human intellect but only by a silent prayer of love that can pierce the *cloud of unknowing*. It urges readers to use a short word and to 'fasten it to your heart. Fix your mind on it permanently, so nothing can dislodge it.'[46]

The 1960s saw a revival of interest in the contemplative tradition in the West. In 1961, Thomas Merton published *The Wisdom of the Desert*, a collection of the famous sayings of the Desert Fathers and Mothers.[47] He practised meditation and considered that 'the deepest level of communication is not talking, but communion. It is wordless. It is beyond words and it is beyond concept'.[48] In the mid-1970s, John Main came across the writings of John Cassian, who, in the early years of the fifth century CE, had chronicled the teachings of the desert monks.[49] Through Cassian's writings he rediscovered the Christian tradition of the Desert Fathers and Mothers and he adapted their method for the modern world, with a view to making it widely available to laypeople, as a twice-daily practice for everyday life. As we have seen, he named it 'Christian meditation'. At the same time, Fr Thomas Keating and others were reviving Christian contemplative practice in the United States and they named it 'Centering Prayer'. There are subtle differences between the practices but they have much in common and, ultimately, share the same desert origins. John Main taught that the practice of meditation was as natural to one's soul as breathing is to the body.[50] Christian meditation is becoming increasingly popular today, a living tradition.[51]

Within the Christian tradition, meditation is not intended to replace other kinds of prayer but is understood as adding a depth of meaning to all prayer. It facilitates the movement from mental to receptive prayer with a view to building a personal relationship of communion with Christ.

Endnotes

1. Maharishi Mahesh Yogi introduced the TM technique and TM movement in India in the mid-1950s and embarked on a series of world tours from 1958 to 1965, promoting and teaching the practice.

2. Jon Kabat-Zinn, *Full Catastrophe Living: Using the Wisdom of Your Body and Mind to Face Stress, Pain and Illness*, New York: Bantam Books, 2013, 1990.

3. Recollection not in the sense of recalling something to memory but in terms of bringing oneself back to a state of composure.

4. See George S. Everly and Jeffrey Lating, M, *A Clinical Guide to the Treatment of Human Stress Response*, New York: Springer, 2013, p. 201.

5. Jim Green, *The Heart of Education: Meditation with Children and Young People*, London: Meditatio – World Community for Christian Meditation, 2016, p. 10.

6. Alexander Wynne, *The Origin of Buddhist Meditation*, New York: Routledge, 2007, p. 4.

7. Han F. de Wit, 'The Case for Contemplative Psychology', *Shambhala Sun*, March 2001. 'For de Wit, this is an inner flourishing that occurs in the depth of our being and manifests itself in how we live our everyday lives.' Henry Jansen and Lucia Hofland-Jensen (trans.), *The Spiritual Path: An Introduction to the Psychology of the Spiritual Traditions*, Pittsburgh, PA: Duquense University Press, 1999, p. 32. De Wit asserts that 'people who travel the contemplative path can no longer be described and explained satisfactorily by conventional psychology.'

8. Kabat-Zinn, *Mindfulness for Beginners*, p. 1. Elsewhere Kabat-Zinn defines it as 'the intentional cultivation of non-judgemental, moment-to-moment awareness'. 'Mindfulness Meditation: What It Is, What It Isn't, and Its Role in Health Care and Medicine' in Y. Haruki, Y. Ishii, and M. Suzuki (eds), *Comparative and Psychological Study on Meditation*, Netherlands: Eburon, 1996, p. 161.

9. Ernie Christie, *Coming Home: A Guide to Teaching Christian Meditation to Children*, Singapore: Medio Media, 2008, p. 44.

10. Shanida Nataraja, *The Blissful Brain: Neuroscience and Proof of the Power of Meditation*, London: Octopus Publishing, 2008, p. 14. This book explores the empirical, scientific research into the benefits of meditation and other mindfulness practices. Nataraja's website, www.blissfulbrain.com, is also a very useful source of information. Medical sites such as the Mayo health clinic in the United States note that

meditation can give you a sense of calm, peace and balance that benefits both your emotional well-being and your overall health. See, for example, www.mayoclinic.org/tests-procedures/meditation/in-depth/meditation/art-20045858

11. See, for example, Jon Kabat-Zinn, *Full Catastrophe Living: Using the Wisdom of Your Body and Mind to Face Stress, Pain and Illness*, London, Random House, 2013. See also Herbert Benson, The Relaxation Response, New York: HarperTorch, 1975, p. 8.

12. Herbert Benson, *Beyond the Relaxation Response*, New York: Berkley Books, 1984, p. 4.

13. See, for example: Nataraja, *The Blissful Brain*, pp. 170–82; Heather Buttle, 'Measuring a Journey without Goal: Meditation, Spirituality, and Physiology', *BioMed Research International*, 2015; Cristiano Crescentini et al., 'Mindfulness-Oriented Meditation for Primary School Children: Effects on Attention and Psychological Well-Being,' *Frontiers in Psychology*, 2016; Jonathan Campion, 'A Review of the Research on Meditation', *The Meditatio Journal: Education*, 1(1), 2011, pp. 29–37; Jonathan Campion and Sharn Rocco, 'Minding the Mind: The Effects and Potential of a School-Based Meditation Programme for Mental Health Promotion', *Advances in School Mental Health Promotion*, 2(1), 2009; Sarah Hennelly, 'The immediate and sustained effects of the .b mindfulness programme on adolescents' social and emotional well-being and academic functioning', Oxford Brookes University, 2011; Katherine Weare, 'Evidence for the Impact of Mindfulness on Children and Young People', University of Exeter, 2012; Martin Dresler et al., 'Non-Pharmacological Cognitive Enhancement', *Neuropharmacology*, 64, 2013.

14. Nataraja, *The Blissful Brain*, p. 204.

15. The research suggests that while there is potential for adverse effects in terms of mental, physical or spiritual well-being, the concerns related mainly to long-term intensive meditation, such as 10-day Vipassana retreats. See Nataraja, *The Blissful Brain*, pp. 182–5. In addition, Lustyk et al. undertook a review of relevant studies in 2009, which addressed research safety and participant screening in respect of studies on mindfulness meditation with a view to addressing areas of difficulty and developing guidelines for researchers. See M.K. Lustyk et al., 'Mindfulness Meditation Research: Issues of Participant Screening, Safety Procedures, and Researcher Training', *Advances in Mind-Body Medicine*, 24(1), 2009, pp. 20–30.

16. Martin Laird, Associate Professor of Theology at Villanova University, PA, in private correspondence with this researcher.

17. Weare, 'Evidence for the Impact of Mindfulness on Children and Young People', p. 4.

18. Laurence Freeman, *Jesus: The Teacher Within*, Norwich: SCM Press, 2010, p. 198.

19. MBSR was developed in the USA in the 1970s by Professor Jon Kabat-Zinn with a view to integrating the practice of mindfulness, including meditation, into the field of medicine. MBSR is a programme that reduces stress by developing mindfulness, meaning it seeks the intentional cultivation of moment-by-moment awareness in a non-judgemental and accepting way. The intervention is free of any cultural, religious and ideological factors, but associated with the Buddhist origins of mindfulness. Participants follow an eight-week programme after which they are asked to continue with the daily exercise by integrating it into their everyday routine. See Andrea Will et al., 'Mindfulness-Based Stress Reduction for Women Diagnosed with Breast Cancer', *Cochrane Database of Systematic Reviews*, 2, 2015.

20. 'Mindfulness-Based Stress Reduction (MBSR) is a well-defined and systematic patient-centred educational approach which uses relatively intensive training in mindfulness meditation as the core of a program to teach people how to take better care of themselves and live healthier and more adaptive lives.' Kabat-Zinn, 'Mindfulness Meditation: What It Is, What It Isn't, and It's Role in Health Care and Medicine', p. 163. The title of one of Kabat-Zinn's earliest books on MBSR, first published in 1990, is *Full Catastrophe Living: How to Cope with Stress, Pain and Illness Using Mindfulness Meditation*, reflecting the initial self-centred intention of the practice for the practitioner. However, it is important to acknowledge that later versions of the programme are more inclusive and participants are invited to be generous towards themselves and others through attentive listening and generating feelings of compassion. Nonetheless, the primary intention of the practice is patient-centred or person-centred i.e. self-centred.

21. Jack Kornfield, *Meditation for Beginners*, Boulder, Colorado: Sounds True, 2004, p. 12. In particular, within the Mahayana Buddhist tradition, the purpose of the practice is not merely enlightenment for the practitioner 'but for the sake of salvation of all sentient beings'. See also Daniel Goleman, *The Meditative Mind: The Varieties of Meditative Experience*, Florence, MA: More Than Sound, 2012, p. 82.

22. I want to stress that by using the phrase centred on the self, I do not mean to suggest that such an approach is selfish, or lacking consideration for other people. My focus here is on the intention

of the tradition, not necessarily of the person adopting any of these practices. For example, a person may well choose to take up Christian meditation for personal spiritual gain but that would not accord with the intention of the tradition. Likewise, I have no doubt that many adopt the practice of secular mindfulness for altruistic reasons – indeed, over recent decades that practice has acknowledged more and more its affinity with Buddhism and the other-centred intention of Buddhist meditation.

23. The paradox of intention may help one to understand how effortless intention can be so productive. Most people have personal experience of this paradox. When one is trying desperately to recall what is on the tip of the tongue, one must let go of the effort to remember and rely on the mysterious power of effortless intention to bring to mind what cannot otherwise be recalled. In other words, one must hold on to the intention to bring the memory to mind while at the same time ceasing all effort to recall it! In similar fashion, the intention the practitioner brings to meditation seems to be equally important and effective in realising its intention.

24. John Main, *In Times of Anxiety*, London: The World Community for Christian Meditation, 2009, p. 13.

25. Laurence Freeman describes mystery as 'the wholeness of reality present at a level of consciousness into which reason and imagination cannot penetrate – and yet it is not an experience that betrays reason or cannot be expressed symbolically.' 'The Contemplative Teacher' in Ernie Christie, *Coming Home: A Guide to Teaching Christian Meditation to Children*, Singapore: Medio Media, 2008, pp. 4–11.

26. Laurence Freeman, 'A Letter from Laurence Freeman', *Christian Meditation Newsletter*, 33(4), 2009.

27. James Finley, *Christian Meditation: Experiencing the Presence of God*, New York: HarperCollins, 2004, p. 54.

28. The understanding of the true-self as one's real essence, while its Christian expression is unique, is also reflected in several Eastern wisdom traditions. For example, Buddhism too stresses the capacity of the individual to see through the illusory, conditioned self to the essence of one's true nature, which leads to an awareness that in its place exists an expansive state of being. Buddhism distinguishes between the 'lesser self' (related to the ego of Western psychology) and the 'greater self,' which is grounded in a deep respect for the dignity of all and the wisdom that perceives the interdependence of life, which understands that human beings 'inter-are' with all of creation. See, for

example, Thich Nhat Hanh, *Interbeing: Commentaries on the Tiep Hien Precepts*, Delhi: Full Circle Publishing, 2003. 'The concept of the true-self is reflected too in the Hindu tradition; for example, the Upanishads speak of the spirit of the one who created the universe as dwelling in the heart of each person and describes this spirit as the one who in silence is loving to all.' John Main, *Moment of Christ: The Path of Meditation*, London: Bloomsbury, 1998, pp. 76–7. This understanding of the true-self gives rise to the mutual Hindu greeting *Namaste* which means, in essence, 'The divine in me recognises the divine in you.' Eckhart Tolle, who writes about the ongoing transformation of human consciousness, describes the dawning spiritual understanding of the illusion of separateness in terms of a deepening empathic and loving awareness: 'Love is a deep empathy with the other's "Beingness." You recognise yourself, your essence, in the other. And so you can no longer inflict suffering on the other.' Eckhart Tolle, *Guardians of Being*, Novato, CA: New World Library, 2009, p. 108.

29. 'The life and teaching of Jesus unfold the process of yielding to the silence of adoration and receiving its transfiguring effects of ordinary life, giving rise to what we think of as morals and ethics. If only we knew how to listen, the behaviours and attitudes he taught are entailed in the silence, in the beholding itself.' Maggie Ross, *Writing the Icon of the Heart: In Silence Beholding*, Abingdon, UK: The Bible Reading Fellowship, 2011, p. 97.

30. The Christian monastic tradition has a four-fold practice called *Lectio Divina*, the last phase of which is contemplation. The first phase lectio, involves mindfully reading a sacred passage, being aware of what is going on within you as you read; in the second step, *meditatio*, one reflects on what one has read and allows the passage to engage your feelings and emotions as well as your mind; a particular word or phrase may speak to you as a result; in the third phase, oratio, one lets go of discursive thinking and simply allows the phrase to resonate in the heart and finally, one enters the phase of contemplatio, where one simply rests in God's presence. The etymology of the word 'contemplation' is related to 'the act of looking at'.

31. Possibly because the spread of Buddhist meditation practice in the West led to the word 'meditation' being used in modern society to refer to what the Christian tradition had always named as 'contemplation'.

32. John Main, *Word into Silence: A Manual for Christian Meditation*, Norwich: Canterbury Press, 2006, p. vii.

33. St Augustine wrote that the whole purpose of this life is to open the

eye of the heart by which we see God. See St Augustine, 'Sermon 38 on the New Testament' in Philip Schaff (ed.), *The Early Church Fathers: Nicene and Post-Nicene Fathers, First Series*, Vol. 6, Buffalo, NY: Christian Literature Publishing Company, 1888.

34. The Hebrew words for heart, *léb* and *lébáb*, occur about 850 times in the Old Testament, very often referring to the heart as the seat of a person's inner being. The Greek word *kardia* occurs around 160 times in the New Testament as a true dynamic equivalent. See Stephen D. Renn, *Expository Dictionary of Bible Words: Word Studies for Key English Bible Words Based on the Hebrew and Greek Texts*, Peabody, MA: Hendrickson Publishers, 2005, p. 476–8.

35. 'For thou has [sic] created us for thyself, and our heart knows no rest, until it may repose in Thee.' St Augustine, *The Confessions of St Augustine*, London: Fontana, 1996, p. 1.

36. Bernadette Flanagan, 'Christian Spirituality and Religious Mysticism: Adjunct, Parallel or Embedded Concepts?' in Marian de Souza, Jane Bone and Jacqueline Watson (eds), *Spirituality Across Disciplines: Research and Practice*, Cham, Switzerland: Springer International Publishing, 2016, p. 21.

37. 'It is older than Christianity itself and was a rich part of the Christian tradition up to medieval times. It is only in our own lifetime that we have woken up to the fact that here in the West for 600 or so years the treasure of pure, silent prayer has been almost completely forgotten and abandoned, even in religious communities.' Benignus O'Rourke, *Finding Your Hidden Treasure: The Way of Silent Prayer*, London: Darton, Longman and Todd, 2010, p. 17.

38. See, for example, Lk 4:42, Lk 6:12, Mk 1:35, Mk 6:45, Mk 14:33, Jn 11:41–2, Mt 15:36 and Mt 14:23.

39. Laurence Freeman, 'Jesus' in Kim Nataraja (ed.), *Journey to the Heart: Christian Contemplation through the Centuries – an Illustrated Guide*, London: Canterbury Press, 2011, p. 20.

40. Christians believe that Jesus has sent the Spirit into every human heart. 'And hope does not put us to shame, because God's love has been poured out into our hearts through the Holy Spirit, who has been given to us' (Rm 5:5).

41. Laurence Freeman, *Your Daily Practice*, Singapore: Medio Media, 2008, p. 10.

42. 'This silence is to be entered, not apprehended.' R. Sardello and C. Sanders-Sardello, *Silence: The Mystery of Wholeness*, Berkeley, California: Goldenstone Press, 2008, p. xvi.

43. The German mystic Meister Eckhart observed, 'God is not found in the soul by adding anything, but by a process of subtraction.' Meister Eckhart, 'Sermon on the Fourth Sunday after Trinity,' in James M. Clark (ed.), *Meister Eckhart: Selected Treatises and Sermons*, London: Faber and Faber, 1958, p. 194.

44. Main, *Word into Silence*, p. 3.

45. While contemplative prayer declined in the West from the 6th Century, it remained a part of the Eastern Orthodox tradition in the form of 'The Jesus Prayer:' 'Lord, Jesus Christ, Have mercy on me, a sinner.' Mark 10:47.

46. Patrick J. Gallacher, ed. *The Cloud of Unknowing*, Teams Middle English Text Series (Kalamazoo, Mich: Western Michigan University Medieval Institute Publications, 1997), 37-38, lines 500-04. Quoted in Carmen Acevedo Butcher, *The Cloud of Unknowing with the Book of Privy Council: A New Translation* (London: Shambala, 2011), Kindle Location 219 of 3794.

47. Thomas Merton, *The Wisdom of the Desert: Sayings from the Desert Fathers of the Fourth Century*, New York: A New Directions Book, 1961. The Desert Fathers and Mothers were early Christian hermits (monks) who lived in the deserts of Egypt from around the third century CE. The communities that grew out of these informal communities later became the model for Christian monasticism.

48. Quoted in Paul Harris, 'John Main and the Practice of Christian Meditation', www.bahaistudies.net/asma/johnmain.pdf, accessed 25 January 2013.

49. Cassian (360–435) had spent some years with the desert monks and later founded an Egyptian-style monastery in southern Gaul, near Marseilles. He was particularly influenced by the writings of Evagrius, one of the Desert Fathers.

50. Freeman, 'Jesus', p. 1.

51. Laurence Freeman notes that 'every time we sit to meditate we enter into a living tradition'. Ibid., p. 20.

Interlude

How to Meditate

Being Still in Body and Mind

Christian meditation is a form of focused-attention meditation. In this form of meditation one sits in silence, with the aim of being still in body and mind; this stillness is brought about through the narrowing of focus to a word or a phrase or the physical sensation of the breath. One's energy is intentionally withdrawn from all objects of attention and placed not so much *on* the word as *in* the word. Every time the meditator becomes aware that their attention has wandered and realises that they are caught up in thoughts or emotions, they gently but firmly bring their attention back to the breath or word, without judgement or frustration, no matter how often. And, believe me, it will be often. As noted, Western traditions tend to focus on a sacred word or mantra rather than the breath. Christian meditation, in the John Main tradition, suggests using the word 'Ma-ra-na-tha', an Aramaic word meaning 'Come, Lord' or 'The Lord has come'.[1] There is nothing magical about the word but it flows easily off the tongue. One says it as if it were four single words, each comprising a consonant and a vowel. And one can appreciate its intentional character without becoming preoccupied with its meaning; because it is an unfamiliar word, it doesn't draw one into thought. Laurence Freeman once asked a group of children to suggest a word for meditation and one young boy suggested 'sausages'. That would not be a good choice because it brings to mind immediately a pan of frying sausages – I can hear them sizzling in the pan and I become distracted immediately!

Because the intention in meditation is to achieve a state of alert relaxation, posture is important. It is very helpful if the back is straight so that the airways are free; otherwise there is a danger that one will nod off. John Main summarised the instructions for meditation as follows:

> Sit down. Sit still and upright. Close your eyes lightly. Sit relaxed but alert. Silently, interiorly begin to say a single word. We recommend the prayer-phrase 'Maranatha'. Recite it as four syllables of equal length. Listen to it as you say it, gently but continuously. Do not think or imagine anything – spiritual or otherwise. If thoughts and images come, these are distractions at the time of meditation, so keep returning to simply saying the word. Meditate each morning and evening for between twenty and thirty minutes.[2]

Although the aim in meditation, to be still in body and mind, is very simple, because the mind is so readily distracted it is very difficult to do. If you have never meditated, now is a good time to get a taste of it. I invite you to put down this book in a moment – for just thirty seconds – and to sit wherever you are with a view to being still in body and mind. In other words, to try, as effortlessly as possible, to sit so that there is no physical movement in your body and no movement of thought in your mind. It will help your understanding if you try this now – just for thirty seconds.

> **Practice One**
> Aim to be still in body and mind
> for the next thirty seconds.

Let's think about how you experienced those few moments. Your intention was to be still in body and mind, so let's reflect on them in turn. Most people find it comparatively easy to be still in body for a short while. When I do this exercise with large groups – whether of adults or children – normally there isn't a sound to be heard within the room. Noises from outside – birds singing, a car passing by, a lawnmower mowing the grass outside – make their presence felt but most people have little difficulty being still in body. Of course, the longer the period of stillness, the greater the challenge. In a twenty-minute meditation, many people find that physical distractions can arise fairly quickly. You may become aware of an itch on your face that demands to be scratched; in fact, when you first start to meditate, the presence of the itch may not arise in your conscious awareness until you realise you have already scratched it. Your first awareness might be noticing that your hand is returning to rest after relieving the itch. All of the traditions suggest it is important to avoid giving in to physical as well as mental distractions, unless it really is necessary; for example, if you suffer from back pain, and it sets in during meditation, then by all means make yourself comfortable before continuing. In any case, by and large, most people find it is relatively easy to be still in body.

By comparison, it is very difficult to be still in mind, even for thirty seconds. It is a simple human tendency that when we sit in stillness, thoughts arise. It is part of the human condition in the modern world that, even when silent, our natural tendency is to stay in our heads. The ego doesn't like to be sidelined, so it makes its presence felt in one way or another. You can be sure that whenever you sit in meditation, thoughts will arise.

In the long run the awareness of this is itself a huge lesson from meditation, because we become aware of how our actions are so often tainted by the nature of our subconscious thoughts. Meditation teaches us that our thoughts are merely events in the field of our awareness, a bit like sports commentary. Ultimately, meditation teaches us how to be in relationship with our thoughts. That is one of the fruits of meditation. Practising meditation, we must accept that as we sit in silence, thoughts will arise unbidden and continuously. They arise from our preoccupations, our desires, our needs, our attachments, our worries, our feelings, our emotions, our fears, our hopes. Initially, it seems impossible to avoid them. We get caught up in our thoughts quickly and without awareness and it is not until our witnessing awareness returns that we realise we have been thinking; we realise that once more a thought or emotion has hooked our attention and distracted us from our intention to be still in mind. But don't despair! Meditation is not about having no thoughts, but returning from them, time after time, to the intention to be still. The distractions occur repeatedly, and that can be very frustrating, if you allow it to be so. The challenge of meditation is to acknowledge and release each thought without entertaining it or being entertained or captured by it.

Have you ever used WhatsApp or a similar app on your phone? Have you learned how difficult it can be to resist its incessant call? I find it can be really annoying when even a small group on WhatsApp start sharing stories. 'Ping' goes your phone, repeatedly – alerting you to a string of new notifications. How easily we give in to the distraction and have a quick glance. Over time one may develop an improved capacity to hear those pings but ignore them until one is on a break. The challenge is the same in meditation – to acknowledge each thought, resist the subtle temptation to 'read' it straight away and learn to let it go gently and immediately.

Acknowledge but Don't Entertain Your Thoughts

That's where the sacred word (or mantra) comes in. The practice, the discipline, is to return to the word gently every time we become aware that we are thinking. It is very important to do so gently. We simply accept that distractions occur, that thoughts will arise, but we choose not to entertain them. And when we 'wake up out of thought', as it were, when we become aware that, yet again, we have been thinking, we simply return to the word and start over. We release our thoughts without judgement or criticism; and that can be difficult because the ego sees a great opportunity here to criticise and get back in on the action. Critical, negative thoughts may surface, but all you have to do is release those thoughts too and start over. You simply start again ... and again ... and again. Meditation is actually about returning to your word which is a symbol of your intention, over and over again.

If you meditate for five, ten or twenty minutes it may feel like you spent most of the time in thought or in a state of continuous distraction. But in between the thoughts and the distractions there will be gaps, imperceptible but real. There will be moments, however brief, of absolute silence. In these gaps thinking ceases and you are simply present. Of course, you will not be aware of them – if you were, you would be thinking. Because of this it is very difficult to describe what happens. Different writers on contemplation have attempted to do so. Maggie Ross describes the process as one of accessing deep mind as distinct from our everyday, self-conscious mind in which we are merely skating on the surface of our consciousness. James Finley suggests that, because we experience so much of our lives through ordinary self-conscious mind, we might be said to spend most of our waking hours living on the outer circumference of the inner richness of our lives. But we can, all of us, access that rich centre, through meditation, through stillness and silence. As we grow in our practice of meditation we learn that silence is not the absence of sound, but the absence of self; it is about the letting go of the ego-self and discovering our true-self in the silence.[3] In the absence of egoic self, we begin to sense an awareness of the real presence, however dimly. The practice of meditation awakens us to the extraordinary in the ordinary.

Meditation with Children

The instructions are simple: Be still in body and mind. But the practice is not easy. And in the short-term nothing seems to be happening. The benefits take time and the fruits even longer. But the practice has the potential to be powerfully transformative. And, remember, whatever happens during your meditation period is just fine. However often you find yourself returning to your attention is fine. It is all about returning, again and again, to sit in silence in the presence of the divine. Every time you catch yourself thinking, let the thought go; release it and return to your sacred word. It is the faithful restructuring of your attention, not the lapsing into thought, that is important.

Practice Two

Now that you have a better understanding of what it means to meditate, set the timer on your phone for four minutes and enjoy a four-minute meditation.[4]

Your aim is to be as still as possible in body and mind for the next four minutes. Your aim is to repeat your word from the start until the end of your meditation; say it slowly and lovingly. Say it silently and yet, listen to it as you say it. Thoughts will arise, but as soon as you become aware of them, you will let them go. You will do that by returning to the word 'Ma-ra-na-tha' (or your own chosen word).

It doesn't matter how many times you have to return to the word. The task is not to have no thoughts. Your task is to return faithfully to your word every time you realise you have become caught up in a thought. If you do thirty push-ups in a gym, you know the repetition is doing you good, strengthening the muscles in your upper arms. Likewise in meditation, the repetition is good for you. It strengthens your 'attention muscle' and helps you to avoid becoming caught up in, captivated by, your thoughts.

You might imagine you are taking a holiday from your thoughts, you are getting out of your own way so your true-self can be awakened.

Endnotes

1. If the two-word formula in the Aramaic is read as 'marana-tha', the meaning 'Come, Lord' is suggested; however, if it is read as 'maran-atha', the interpretation 'The Lord has come' is indicated. Personally, I prefer the second interpretation because it accords with the understanding that Jesus is always present in our lives and that it is we who make ourselves present to his presence in meditation.

2. Main, *Word into Silence*, p. xvii.

3. Anthony de Mello, *One Minute Wisdom*, Anand, India: Gujarat Sahitya Prakash, 1985, p. 142.

4. Alternatively, the website www.christianmeditation.ie has soundfiles in the meditation with children section which can be used to time your session.

Chapter Two

The Fruits of Meditation

Introduction

In the last chapter, we explored the benefits of meditation. I use the word 'benefits' to describe the practical, pragmatic, down-to-earth outcomes of meditation – the physical, psychological, emotional and cognitive gains. But the wisdom and religious traditions of the world claim that the practice of meditation also contributes to human flourishing and I refer to this deeper, inner flourishing as the fruits of the practice.

The Fruits of Meditation According to the Wisdom Traditions

Psychologists have long been aware that the meditative traditions claim to contain psychological insights and knowledge about humankind and the spiritual development of people. In recent decades, the field of contemplative psychology has been developed to understand and describe how meditation gives rise to personal and communal insight.[1] It identifies three key fruits of meditation: firstly, meditation awakens us to the validity and value of perceptual knowledge; secondly, through meditation we come to realise how our thinking, our attachments and our conditioning colour and distort our perception and we learn to see more accurately; thirdly, we begin to apprehend that meditation transforms our sense of self-identity.

Meditation Awakens us to the Value of Perceptual (Spiritual) Knowledge

The psychiatrist and author Larry Culliford notes:

> Contemplation [meditation] soon reveals that there are
> different kinds of knowledge. What can be observed,
> measured and tested gives rise to scientific [conceptual]
> knowledge; but there is also the knowledge of how to be
> and behave, of how to grow and mature throughout life.
> This is wisdom or spiritual knowledge.[2]

Many consider it to be a shortcoming of conventional psychology that its image of the human being ignored the spiritual perspective.[3] Conventional psychology takes a profane view of the individual and posits that body and mind are experienced as two different entities, while in the meditative traditions and in contemplative psychology, 'body and mind gradually come to be seen as two experiential qualities of one human existence.'[4] We saw in chapter one that the Western world is dominated by left-brain thinking, resulting in a bias towards rational thought, towards conceptual knowledge, so that the Western mindset tends to deny the validity of perceptual knowledge. Yet, the two ways of seeing the world, the profane and the sacred, lead to two distinct ways of knowing, both of which are equally valid.[5]

As we meditate, the repeated pattern of letting go of thoughts makes us keenly aware of the thinker and of our capacity to witness the thinker and we find that a higher level of consciousness has become activated. The realisation dawns that 'there is a vast realm of intelligence beyond thought, [and] that thought is only a tiny aspect of that intelligence. You also realise that all the things that truly matter – beauty, love, creativity, joy, inner peace – arise from beyond the mind. You begin to awaken.'[6] Not everything can be known conceptually; not everything can be explained in words. There is a language of the heart, the language of silence. Perceptual knowledge is intuitive, it arises from being calmly present to reality and it requires no mental processing. The renowned psychologist Robert Romanyshyn argues that because the natural and the human sciences are very different fields of enquiry, they require different ways of knowing. For example, a person cannot fully explain a historical event or a work of art or a dream in the same way or with the same precision that one can a scientific experiment.

The regular practice of meditation leads to an appreciation of the validity and value of perceptual knowledge. The meditator comes to know that 'mystery can indeed be known without being solved ... without being understood'.[7] The meditative mindset holds back from labelling or categorising so it can see things as they are, whole in themselves. This is a form of first-person knowledge, as against third-person knowledge.[8] Perceptual knowledge does not replace or displace conceptual knowledge – they are both necessary. However, in the Western world today conceptual knowledge has displaced perceptual knowledge. Conceptual knowledge is dualist. It operates primarily on an either/or basis. It analyses, separates and differentiates rather than integrates. It struggles to comprehend any experience that cannot be conceptualised and described in words and images. By comparison, the Eastern mindset seems to incorporate a non-dual perspective, tending to understand the mind and body as integrated, as a psycho-physical unity that is innately spiritual in essence. The non-dual mindset represents a move away from seeing through differentiation (*either* this *or* that) to perceiving reality as a single unified field. It operates on a both/and basis. It is comfortable with unknowing and remains open to ambiguity, paradox and possibility.

The rational mindset tends to disregard perceptual knowledge, seeing it as irrational. However, others reject the charge, insisting that perceptual knowledge is pre-rational, rational and trans-rational all at once. Both ways of knowing, the conceptual and the perceptual, are necessary for abundant, holistic living. The combination of conceptual and perceptual knowledge gives rise to a more balanced way of knowing.[9]

Although the Western world tends to deny the validity of perceptual knowledge as an expression of the spiritual, it does have an appreciation of the potential of the arts to give expression to that which cannot be easily expressed. When we attempt to describe the ineffable through prose, the danger is that we may confuse the words for the truth they are pointing towards. As the ancient proverb expresses it, 'When the wise man points to the moon, the fool sees only the finger.'[10] If the words we use substitute themselves for the phenomenon that they are attempting to describe, the attempt fails to capture and communicate the wisdom we are trying to express. Put simply, the word is not the thing it describes. Words are merely stepping stones toward the thing they strive to reveal.

So, we need art, symbol and poetry to communicate truths that are beyond words, to reveal knowledge beyond concepts. The little verse that follows captures this truth well:

> No tongue can tell Your secret
> For the measure of the word obscures Your nature.
> But the gift of the [heart]
> Is that it hears
> What the tongue cannot tell.[11]

Heidegger saw poetry as language in service of the unsayable and the artist Francis Bacon claimed that the job of the artist is always to deepen our intimate connection with mystery, which cannot easily be expressed.[12] Likewise, meditation does not explain, but it deepens our encounter with mystery. Within the religions of the world, theology attempts to do the same job but through concepts. The contemplative traditions assert that the language for expressing and exploring the spiritual quest is silence. Jerome Berryman paraphrases Robert Frost to make the point:

> Our words dance around in a ring and suppose
> While Silence sits in the middle and knows.[13]

Those who practise meditation find that it helps them to enter more deeply into the mystery of their own inner selves, to leave themselves open and vulnerable to unselfconscious engagement with mystery. Every time we slip back from deep mind into self-consciousness, we make our way back to the threshold by letting go, by a willing release of self-conscious activity; we do so by returning to our word, with the intention of dropping without effort into deep mind once again, although we will only ever be dimly aware it has happened when self-consciousness arises once again. Over time, we begin to discern the potential depths of perceptual knowledge and our trust in the process deepens, as does our obscure experiential understanding of the joy of pure being. We discover that joy is not something to be achieved, not something to be possessed but a natural condition that already possesses us.

Discerning the depths of perceptual knowing as we sit in silence might be compared to our eyesight adjusting to see in the dark. When we enter a dark room from bright daylight, the pupil of our eye dilates; it opens wider to allow in more light so that we can see better in the darker environment. We know from experience that it will take time for our eyesight to adjust and that if we wait patiently, we will begin to see much more clearly in the darker environment. This analogy helps us to understand what happens as we sit in silence, still in body and mind. Our consciousness adjusts to the silence and we find that we can sense things we are not normally aware of; our left-brain conceptual faculties take a step back and our right-brain perceptual faculties take a step forward and we become receptive to perceptual as well as conceptual knowledge.

Many of the Desert Fathers from the early Christian tradition of meditation developed profound insights into the practice, suggesting that non-dual consciousness was achieved by 'putting the mind into the heart'.[14] It is the rational mind that creates the abyss between conceptual and perceptual knowledge but it is the heart that crosses it. John Main expressed this idea when he said that meditation moves the centre of gravity of the person from the head to the heart. This has the capacity to lead the meditator towards a state of objectless awareness and transcendence of the egoic self as one's mindset is transformed by being places in the heart. The resulting non-dual perspective is comfortable with uncertainty and paradox and is open to the mysterious.[15]

Both ways of knowing – the conceptual and the perceptual – are important; they complement one another, counteracting each other's shortcomings.[16] Together they unite head and heart, intellect and intuition; they awaken and nourish one's innate humaneness and lead to compassionate action. But they can only do so when the validity and value of perceptual knowledge are acknowledged. It is a key fruit of meditation that it gives rise to this insight.

Meditation Improves our Clarity of Perception

On a very practical level, meditators come to understand how their thoughts and conditioning colour their experience and distort their clarity of perception. We have seen how, when one sits in silence, even with the intention of being still in body and mind, thoughts arise involuntarily. The regular practice of meditation draws attention, often infuriatingly, to the constant, futile, mental agitation that is an inevitable part of the human capacity for thinking. As one sits in the silence and stillness of meditation, the only movement is the involuntary stream of thought that invariably arises. The practitioner begins to meditate by focusing his or her attention on a single object and as soon as he or she notices that they have been caught up in thoughts, they direct their attention back to the chosen focal point, without judgement or emotion but gently, with great patience. Every time they do this, they are conscious of having escaped from these thoughts and become (even fleetingly) aware of their content. For that moment at least, they dis-identify from their thoughts and are no longer imprisoned or captivated by them – they have objectified them. They come to realise that they are not their thoughts, feelings or emotions – that the thoughts have merely arisen in their consciousness. They learn at a very deep level that their thoughts do not define who they are. The unpredictable movement of the mind is made visible because of the stability that is offered by the stillness and silence of meditation. The meditator comes to understand at a very deep level the value of standing back and taking time for stillness and silence before responding to situations in life. Meditation changes our relationship with our thoughts and our habitual patterns of thought. One learns that while thoughts can be helpful, they can also, at times, be very misleading. Freedom from being imprisoned by our thoughts is a very great freedom. Meditation promotes a growing capacity for awareness of thought and the importance of one's relationship with thought.

Over time practitioners make valuable discoveries about their thoughts: they learn that thoughts arise involuntarily and continuously and that the stream of thoughts has a very compelling nature. They also learn how readily human beings identify themselves with their thoughts and they learn that this is ultimately an illusion. I am using the word 'thoughts' here in a wide-ranging sense to include the mental acknowledgement of ideas, words, feelings, emotions, sensations and so on. Regularly practising meditation sharpens one's ability to distinguish between seeing one's thoughts and being caught up in thought. You come to recognise, as a thought passes through your mind, that it is a just thought and you realise that the important thing is not the absence of thoughts, but not allowing yourself to be imprisoned by them. Practising meditation leads to a dawning awareness that what we regard to be a true experience of reality is very often distorted by the noise of our thoughts, fears, desires, attachments and conditioning. In other words, we become aware how often our thoughts act like a filter, colouring and distorting reality and how often we react inappropriately to situations because of those distortions. We grow in awareness of how our thoughts condition our unfolding experience of life and what we tell ourselves about it. We learn that we are so much more than the story we construct about ourselves. We learn that our level of wakefulness, of self-awareness, can rise and fall as if it is on a dimmer switch and the more we become lost in thought, the more it dims. We come to realise that when such wakefulness is at a low ebb, very often we react to situations out of our own need when the situation actually calls for us to respond to the needs of another. This is an important fruit of meditation. It cultivates wakefulness as a vital aspect of human experience. Practised regularly, meditation keeps us at a higher level of self-awareness so that our fixation on our egocentric, conceptualised experience becomes unravelled and slowly but surely dissolves. This realisation dawns not conceptually but experientially as we learn to release thoughts without engaging with them. We realise we are developing the capacity to set aside the narratives of our mind and the habitual reactions those narratives generate.

This, then, is a second inner fruit of meditation: we come to recognise how, if we are not self-aware, our thinking makes us the author of our own 'reality' which is, in fact, distorted. As meditation raises and maintains our level of self-awareness, keeping the dimmer switch open to full power, we begin to comprehend our actions, interactions and relationships more accurately, more clearly. Our heightened clarity of perception leads ultimately to responsive compassionate action in the world. Indeed, the wisdom traditions regard one's growing capacity for contemplative action (including speech) as the only true indicator of one's progress in meditation practice.

Meditation Transforms Our Sense of Self-Identity

As we grow and mature through life, our sense of who we are develops and changes. At any given point in time, each of us will have a sense of identity that we think defines us. Our sense of self-identity will depend on our upbringing, our family, our society, our level of education, our life experience and our current circumstances. It also depends on our level of consciousness.

Ken Wilber proposed a model for understanding the development of consciousness in human beings. He depicted it as a progressive movement through levels (or structures) of consciousness that is linked to the growth of individuals along a range of human capacities such as cognitive development, emotional development and so on. He used the colours of the rainbow to describe the different levels, showing how each stage builds on and incorporates the previous one. Once we have mastered a particular stage, we are ready to move to the next level when the circumstances are right.[17]

As individuals grow from childhood to adulthood and on to old age, they move through the stages of consciousness but not all at the same pace and not always through all of the stages. Very few people ever reach the top of any line of development; for example, only a very small percentage of the world's athletes reach the zenith of their sport. The same applies to growth in one's level of consciousness. Each level of consciousness represents how a person habitually interprets their life experience and each level embodies a different world view.[18] If we limited our description to just three broad levels of human consciousness, they might be described as ego-centric (where everything is seen to revolve around the needs of the individual), ethno-centric (where one's family, ethnicity or nationality is seen to hold centre stage) or world-centric (where everything is considered in light of our common, multi-cultural humanity and our joint responsibility for stewardship of the earth).

It is important to stress that very many people are typically unaware of their stage of consciousness. Because it is the lens through which they interpret the world, from their perspective this is simply how things are – there is no other way of seeing it. The dominant culture of a society – its generally accepted way of interpreting the world – can make it difficult for individuals to grow beyond that common way of seeing. But as one grows through levels of consciousness, one becomes aware that there are, in fact, other perspectives and one develops the capacity to incorporate a more objective view of reality, to examine one's subjective personal experience in the light of external and objective perspectives. Irish society today looks back with horror at the treatment meted out by an earlier Irish society to unmarried mothers and their children who were inhumanely institutionalised; in the same way, Irish society in fifty years' time may be at a loss to understand our current treatment of refugee families that are institutionalised in the appalling confined conditions of 'direct provision'. The growth of human rights, women's rights and children's rights are all related to changing levels of consciousness across whole societies, which are reflective of changes of consciousness at an individual level. The movement through levels of consciousness happens gradually as we grow and mature over the years, but sometimes quite suddenly as we experience an 'Aha!' moment that opens us up to more subtle ways of knowing and relating to the world. As we move through the stages of consciousness, our world view changes and we begin to realise that our perception of reality is relative to our current stage of consciousness development. Typically, each new level of consciousness is less egocentric than the previous one; each new level gives rise to a wider perspective, a broader way of seeing the world and one's relationship to it and to others.

Meditation promotes growth through levels of consciousness.[19] It makes us more deeply aware that our interpretation of our internal and external landscapes is merely one perspective and that other perspectives are possible and may be more accurate. The practitioner begins to understand that what he or she experiences as reality, and names as reality, is, in fact, a relative reality and that there are other, equally valid, ways of seeing the world. This makes us more tolerant, compassionate and responsive.

At any given stage of life, we are at particular stage of consciousness. Because we have gone through the previous stages, they are recognisable and have become integrated into the current stage. But, if we get stuck at a particular level of consciousness – as many do – we may become very fundamentalist in our views and may not be able to see beyond our own egocentric concerns. A lack of awareness of any stages not yet experienced creates distrust of and wariness towards those who have made the transition. Indeed, it can be scary to hear a different viewpoint expressed from a level of consciousness not yet experienced.

One's sense of identity is very much linked to the level of consciousness one occupies. As meditation promotes growth through levels of consciousness, one's sense of identity is transformed. In that sense, one can say that meditation 'broadens the mind' and may be experienced by the person as a more expansive sense of being that leads to a different sense of relating to the world. Meditation waters the seeds of our fundamental humanity. Of course, the fruits of any activity take time to materialise, just as seeds take time to grow. It is important to stress that the wisdom traditions agree that the fruits of meditation arise from and depend on practising meditation regularly, ideally twice daily for twenty to thirty minutes, morning and evening.

The religious traditions of the world speak of such inner human flourishing in terms of the spirit and maintain that meditation has the capacity to nourish the innate spirituality of the individual. The final section of this chapter explores how the fruits of meditation are described in the Christian tradition.

The Fruits of Meditation According to the Christian Tradition

We saw in chapter one that the practice of Christian meditation was revived from the 1960s onwards, a renewal inspired in particular by the work of Thomas Merton, John Main and Thomas Keating. Since then, Laurence Freeman has animated the spread of the practice through his work as director of the World Community for Christian Meditation, while others such as Richard Rohr, Cynthia Bourgeault, Martin Laird and Tilden Edwards have also promoted the contemplative practice in the Christian tradition. That tradition gives a particular expression to the fruits of meditation.

John Main observes, as do the wisdom traditions, that meditation teaches us detachment from self-preoccupation, from a mindset that puts oneself at the centre of all creation.

Instead, every time we meditate we become wholly present in the moment, 'we enter into the eternal now of God'.[20] Main writes:

> In the Christian vision of meditation, the whole purpose of this process is to free your spirit to be open to infinity, to allow your heart and your mind, your whole being, to expand beyond all the barriers of your own isolated self and to come into union with all. With the All; with God.[21]

He goes on to say that reality is simply being grounded in God, who is the ground of our being, and that one learns, in the stillness and silence, 'to accept ourselves as we are'. Thomas Merton designated the essence of the human spirit in terms of what he called 'the true-self'. He described it as follows, 'Underlying the subjective experience of the individual self, there is an immediate experience of Being ... [which] is totally different from the experience of self-consciousness.'[22] Expressing this more simply, one might say that there is in each of us a divine spark, which is our true essence, and which is intimately related to the divine.[23] Richard Rohr describes the true-self succinctly as 'who we are in God and who God is in us'.[24] Karl Rahner expressed it in his own unique way, suggesting that as one grows and develops, it is in the unfolding of one's personal history that one simply realises what one already is.[25] The Christian tradition, then, holds that the practice of meditation results in a mysterious 'restructuring of consciousness'[26] that gives rise to an abiding awareness of the true-self and in living life from that perspective. This abiding awareness of the presence of God is acknowledged as a core characteristic across the various strands of Christian mysticism.[27]

As we deepen our practice of meditation we begin to notice that somehow 'our spirit is expanding, our heart is opening, we are becoming more generous. And the change in us comes about because, in meditation, we encounter the power to make this change possible.'[28] In the Christian tradition, meditation is seen as leading to the fruits of the Spirit, which are described in Galatians (5:22) as love, joy, peace, forbearance, kindness, goodness, faithfulness, gentleness and self-control. We discover that, 'The Spirit of him who created the universe dwells in our hearts, and in silence is loving to all.'[29] When we discover the truth of that for ourselves we are truly transfigured, we see the world and all of creation differently and we begin to live out of that perceptual knowledge in a deeply personal way. We become like the Good Samaritan. We realise that it is the quality of our presence in every moment, our awareness of who we truly are, that informs our response to all that we encounter in life. As Laurence Freeman expresses it, 'Conversion, then as now, is not just a matter of changing your opinions or acquiring a new spiritual credit card. It is a revolution in the deep structures of the personality that, if it is genuine, goes on for the rest of your life.'[30] Meditation can lead to a deep sense of inner spaciousness, and we may come to think of it as a place we go to in meditation; however, over time, we come to understand it is, in fact, our true essence, a place we come from, the source of goodness that informs and transforms our way of seeing and being in the world. We experience this spaciousness as the true-self, the location of our deepest sense of who we really are, the site of our defining true-self-identity, of our 'unbounded, flowing sense of selfhood'.[31]

While the Christian tradition has its own unique way of describing the practice and the fruits of meditation, it, nonetheless, incorporates the three aforementioned fruits of meditation: that meditation helps us to appreciate the validity and value of perceptual, spiritual knowledge; it alerts us to the fact that our thinking colours and distorts our clarity of perception; and it teaches us that our perception of reality and our sense of self-identity is relative to our current stage of consciousness. It helps us to break out of our cultural conditioning and frees us from being imprisoned by it. The Christian tradition suggests that meditation contributes to an integration of the psyche, assimilating the profane and sacred world views. As Laurence Freeman observes:

> Deep in the modern psyche there is a split between the sacred and the secular. It affects religious people no less than those who reject all belief. The consequence of this divided psyche is a split vision of reality ... Meditation heals the terrible wound that seems to cut off such large parts of our life from the healing and vivifying power of the sacred.[32]

It is clear from this discussion that all of these traditions, including the Christian, point to deep inner fruits that lead to human flourishing at the level of the individual and society. Ultimately it can lead to awakened, aware, contemplative action that is responsive, not reactive; vibrant, not half-hearted; holistic, not fragmented; and other-directed, not ego-driven.

Both the wisdom traditions and the Christian practice also caution that, while they will in time be experienced in one's daily living, the fruits of meditation do not manifest as rewarding subjective experiences during every time of meditation. The place to look for results is not in what happens during meditation, but after; and not immediately afterwards, nor the following day, but in the longer term.

The fruits of meditation from a Christian perspective might be summed up diagrammatically as shown in Figure 2.1. Meditation validates spiritual knowledge, improves our clarity of perception, transforms our sense of identity and, ultimately, inspires authentic compassionate living. At their heart lies the realisation of the true-self, the understanding that the Divine is not just at the centre of all existence, but lies also at the core of each person.

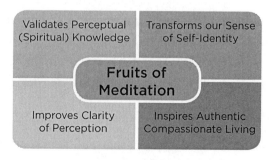

Figure 2.1 The Fruits of Meditation

The Fruits of Meditation

Those who meditate discover not just who they truly are but also who others really are. They discover that Jesus' invitation to love one's neighbour as oneself does not mean to love one's neighbour as much as one loves oneself, but to love one's neighbour who is ultimately one with oneself in God. As Julian of Norwich expressed it, 'The love of God creates in us such a oneing that when it is truly seen, no person can separate themselves from another person.'[33] They discover the ultimate unity of all reality and that it is possible to live joyfully, purposefully and lovingly outside the stream of one's egocentric reality. Meditation slowly but surely reveals the true-self, so it becomes the centre, the lens through which life is lived. When the centre of gravity of our consciousness moves from the head to the heart, we begin to see more clearly, with greater accuracy, and any action we take becomes responsive not reactive, because we begin to live from this new centre. The dualist perspective that splits the world into things that are 'mine' and 'not mine' dissolves into a more unitive way of seeing. One becomes less and less of a mystery to oneself as one develops first-hand self-knowledge. One realises that this is the space in which one's fundamental humanity is grounded and that it gives access to a rich and deep reality. As John Main expressed it, 'In meditation we discover both who we are and why we are.'[34]

From a Christian perspective, we can say that meditation brings about a new way of seeing that leads to a new way of being in the world, informed by the Spirit, which lies at the centre of our being. Commonly we greet people by asking,

Meditation with Children

'How is the world treating you?' We rarely hear the inverse question, 'How are you treating the world?' Meditation makes us keenly aware of how we are treating the world and how this impacts our relationships and all that we encounter. It gives rise to more authentic living, to more compassionate, responsive action for the good of all. Meditation, as a daily practice, is both the seed and fruit of our deepest authenticity. It promotes an authentic inner spiritual life by watering that seed on a daily basis.

In my interviews with the children about their experience of meditation, one child made a simple mistake several times. On three different occasions while explaining how meditation helped her, she referred to it as 'medication'. She is a lovely, good-natured young girl and we chuckled at her mistake each time. But it made me think that in many ways meditation is as effective as medication for many of our ills. Meditation heals us. It restores us to wholeness. Health, however, is not just the absence of problems, pains or disabilities, but health is 'our capacity for wholeness, in which everything including illness or disability can and must be integrated', including the very things that we find most undesirable and may even fear, such as chronic illness, physical or mental suffering and failure.[35] To be truly whole we need to accept that sickness and suffering, even death, are part of the human condition and acknowledge that the tendency not to accept this is unwholesome. In other words, meditation promotes wholeness, which is the truest definition of health. Meditation, then, is a truly healthy practice, which leads toward integration of all the human faculties, to the integration of body, mind and spirit; it is a holistic practice that contributes toward living life abundantly.

How Do These Fruits Flow from Meditation?

As we saw in the previous chapter, Maggie Ross distinguishes between self-conscious mind and deep mind. The left hemisphere of the brain seems to be linked to our everyday self-conscious mind and the right hemisphere to the deep mind. While our neurological understanding of the power of meditation to give rise to rich benefits and deep fruits may increase over the coming decades, Ross helps our metaphorical understanding of how meditation can give access to the deep mind through the very practical example of the 'paradox of intention'. We all know the feeling of having something on the tip of our tongue but being unable to bring it to mind. We know we know it but we cannot bring it to self-consciousness. And most of us discover that in those circumstances the trick to bringing it to mind is first letting it go. That is, of course, paradoxical – the way to remember it is to forget about it! Yet everybody learns sooner or later that it works. Holding on to the intention to recall something while, at the same time, letting go of all effort to do so seems counter-intuitive and irrational but it actually works. When we let go of the striving but gently hold to the intention, our faith – that what we seek will surface in its own time – is rewarded.

Meditation works in a similar way. We hold on to the intention to be still in God's presence, to become 'aware' of that presence at a very deep level of consciousness but in a way that lies beyond self-consciousness. Letting go of all

85

effort while holding on to the intention enables us to wait in unknowing, receptively, without striving, without expectation of a self-conscious experience, having faith that something vital is happening at a very deep level of consciousness. I noted in chapter one that the Irish word for contemplation is *rinnfheitheamh*, which translates literally as 'waiting at the edge'. It captures beautifully and remarkably well that sense of waiting in unknowing. And waiting in unknowing works, although we can never be self-consciously aware of it. It is impossible to articulate what has gone on in deep mind except from the traces it leaves behind.[36] Consequently, one can only point towards the truth of such activity – one can never adequately describe it. But we come to know it works because it bears rich fruit in our lives.

Ross argues that it is our capacity to rest in unknowing that restores the natural flow between the direct knowledge of the deep mind, and our self-conscious thinking.[37] It is by working with silence that we can enliven the flow between the self-conscious mind – which dominates, and distorts, our lives – and the clarity and wisdom of the deep mind, opening us to perceptual knowledge.[38] Although not referring to meditation, Patrick Kavanagh, a deeply contemplative poet, described this truth in his own way:

> … God cannot catch us
> Unless we stay in the unconscious room
> Of our hearts. We must be nothing,
> Nothing that God can make us something.[39]

The fruits of meditation flow from the practice, but in the end, we must accept that it is a graced mystery. Meditation leads to a deepening of consciousness, to a rich inner flourishing that in turn gives rise to contemplative action as the ultimate fruit of meditation. And we recognise too that ongoing responsive contemplative action also produces the seeds of its own flourishing – in a virtuous cycle. And, as the children observed, meditation waters the seeds. The fruit is in the seed that keeps on giving. Meditation mysteriously nourishes the seed and brings it to fruition. Jesus describes the kingdom in this way, as like a seed planted in the soil:

> He leaves it to grow as he goes to bed at night and rises in the morning. All the time it grows 'how he does not know'. But grow it does and in time and by stages the growth becomes visible until it reaches fullness and then harvest. (Mk 4:26–8)

Through the regular practice of meditation, you sense the possibility of an unbounded non-dual selfhood, of participation in divine consciousness; you find yourself drawn towards an experience of apophatic intimacy, although words will fail to describe adequately what you intuit. But you come to understand that meditation moves the centre from which you draw your energy away from conceptual self-conscious mind, in the direction of spacious, perceptual, deep mind.[40] You no longer derive your sense of who you are from what your self-conscious mind tells you about yourself. You are free to be yourself, to be true to yourself, to be your true-self.

Every time you return to the world after meditation you do so revitalised, reenergised, having drawn from the deep well of the Spirit. And you 'know' that you can live your life from that centre. You understand that the only way to solve the problems of the world, whether in your own relationships, your own locality or around the world, is to be part of the answer. Meditation gives you the courage to be true to who you really are, to 'be' an answer.

Practice Three

Now that you have a better understanding of what it means to meditate, why not set the timer on your phone to eight minutes and enjoy an eight-minute meditation.

Follow the instructions in practice two (page 62), extending your period of meditation to eight minutes.

Endnotes

1. Han F. de Wit, 'On Contemplative Psychology' (paper presented at the The Third Symposium on the Psychology of Religion in Europe), Amsterdam, 1986, p. 82. De Wit names James, 1902; Jung, 1939; Clark, 1958; Leuba, 1972; Ornstein, 1972; Podvoll, 1982; Wilber, 1984.

2. Larry Culliford, *The Psychology of Spirituality: An Introduction*, London: Jessica Kingsley Publishers, 2011, p. 46.

3. Over the course of the twentieth century, Western society developed into a distinctly psychological culture. Entire generations in our culture have grown up with the concept of humanity that was drawn up by Freud and they interpreted their experiences by means of this concept. These concepts give shape to our understanding of what it means to be human. See Han F. de Wit, *The Spiritual Path: An Introduction to the Psychology of the Spiritual Traditions*, Henry Jansen and Lucia Hofland-Jensen (trans), Pittsburgh, PA.: Duquense University Press, 1999, p. 23–5.

4. Han F. de Wit, *Contemplative Psychology*, Marie Louise Baird (trans.), Pittsburgh, PA: Dubuesne University Press, 1991, p. 10. It is important to note, however, that while contemplative psychology is based on a spiritual image of the human being, nonetheless, it is *not theocentric* but, like conventional psychology, *anthropocentric* because its central question is 'what happens psychologically to people in their thoughts, words and deeds when they walk the contemplative path?'

5. Two medieval Christian philosophers, Hugh (eleventh century) and Richard of St Victor (twelfth century) spoke of three different ways of seeing: through the eye of the flesh (through sight), the eye of reason (through discursive reflection), and the intuitive eye of true understanding (through meditation/contemplation). See Richard Rohr Daily Meditations, 29 June 2017, cac.org/the-third-eye-2017-06-29/

6. Eckhart Tolle, *The Power of Now: A Guide to Spiritual Enlightenment* (Novato, CA: New World Library, 2010), 17.

7. Gerald May, *Will and Spirit: A Contemplative Psychology*, New York: HarperCollins, 1987, p. 30.

8. Bertrand Russell referred to third-person knowledge as 'knowledge about' something while he regarded first-person knowledge as 'knowledge by acquaintance'. See Bertrand Russell, *The Problems of Philosophy*, London: Oxford University Press, 1912.

9. See, for example, Jack Finnegan, *The Audacity of Spirit: The Meaning and Shaping of Spirituality Today*, Dublin: Veritas, 2008, p. 33.

10. A version of this saying is quoted in Anthony de Mello, *One Minute Nonsense*, Anand, India: Gujarat Sahitya Prakash, 1992, p. 131.

11. Hakim Sanai, 'No Tongue Can Tell Your Secret' in *The Book of Everything: Journey of the Hearts Desire*, Kansas: Andrews McMeel Publishing, 2002. However, I have adapted it by replacing the word 'ear' in the middle line with the word 'heart'.

12. Chessick writes that Heidegger considered that the poet 'responds to the call of Being; he engages in a docile readiness for the Holy which discloses itself to the poet ... [and the poet responds] by forming this address into words [so that] the poet names the Holy.' Richard D. Chessick, 'The Effect of Heidegger's Pathological Narcissism on the Development of His Philosophy' in *Mimetic Desire: Essays on Narcissism in German Literature from Romanticism to Postmodernism*, Jeffrey Adams and Eric Williams (eds), Columbia, SC: Camden House, 1995, p. 112.

13. Jerome W. Berryman, 'Silence Is Stranger Than It Used to Be' in *The Search for a Theology of Childhood: Essays by Jerome W. Berryman from 1978–2009*, Brendan Hyde (ed.), Ballarat, Victoria: Modotti Press, 2013, Kindle location 1940 of 4876. Frost had written a couplet entitled 'The Secret Sits', first published in A Witness Tree, that reads: 'We dance round in a ring and suppose,/But the Secret sits in the middle and knows.' Robert Frost, A Witness Tree, New York: Henry Holt & Co., 1942.

14. Cynthia Bourgeault describes the process of reaching this state of awareness as a rewiring of consciousness that results in an altered 'operating system' that appreciates the value of perceptual knowledge. See Cynthia Bourgeault, *The Heart of Centering Prayer: Nondual Christianity in Theory and Practice*, Boulder, CO: Shambala, 2016, Kindle location 184 of 4494.

15. Ibid., Kindle location 589 of 4494.

16. Han F. de Wit, 'On the Methodology of Clarifying Confusion' in *Current Issues in Theoretical Psychology*, William J. Baker et al. (ed.), Amsterdam: Elsevier Science Publishers BV, 1987, p. 47. De Wit observes also that the awareness strategy clarifies for us whatever arises on stage: our sights, sounds, smells, taste, touch and thoughts, our conceptual knowledge and how all of these intermingle. Conversely, because this clarification has no language, we need to make use of our conceptual strategies to be able to give expression to the truth we have discovered.

17. The movement through the stages should not be understood as rigid rungs on a ladder but as fluid waves of unfolding; like the colours of a rainbow, they flow into one another.

18. Wilber names and describes his stages of consciousness as follows: Infrared (archaic, sensorimotor); Magenta (magical-animistic); Red (egocentric, power, magic-mythic); Amber (mythic, ethnocentric, traditional); Orange (rational, world-centric, pragmatic, modern); Green (pluralistic, multicultural, postmodern); Teal (beginning integral, systemic); Turquoise (global mind); Indigo (illumined mind); Violet (Meta-mind). Wilber sometimes suggests two further stages: Ultra-Violet and Clear Light. Ken Wilber, *Integral Spirituality: A Startling New Role for Religion in the Modern and Postmodern World*, Boston: Integral Books, 2006, p. 251.

19. Ibid., pp. 11, 196.

20. John Main, *The Hunger for Depth and Meaning: Learning to Meditate with John Main*, Singapore: Medio Media, 2007, Kindle location 1378 of 2309.

21. Ibid., Kindle location 1400 of 2309.

22. Thomas Merton, *Zen and the Birds of Appetite*, New York: New Directions Publishing, 1968, p. 24.

23. Robert Browning pointed to the same thing when he wrote, 'There is an inmost centre in us all, where truth abides in fullness.' Robert Browning, 'Paracelsus' in *The Oxford Book of English Mystical Verse*, D.H.S Nicholson and A.H.E. Lee (eds), Oxford: Clarendon Press, 1917, p. 173.

24. Richard Rohr, *Immortal Diamond: The Search for Our True Self*, London: SPCK Publishing, 2013, p. 16. Merton expressed it as follows: 'The secret of my identity is hidden in the love and mercy of God. But whatever is in God is really identical with Him, for His infinite simplicity admits no division and no distinction. Therefore, I cannot hope to find myself anywhere except in Him.' Thomas Merton, *New Seeds of Contemplation*, New York: A New Directions Book, 1961, pp. 37–8.

25. Mary Ann Hinsdale, '"Infinite Openness to the Infinite": Karl Rahner's Contribution to Modern Catholic Thought on the Child' in *The Child in Christian Thought*, Marcia J. Bunge (ed.), Grand Rapids, Michigan: Wm. B. Eerdmans Publishing Co., 2001, Kindle location 7297 of 12703.

26. Thomas Keating, *Open Mind, Open Heart: The Contemplative Dimension of the Gospel*, New Your: Continuum, 2003, p. 4.

27. Bernard McGinn, *The Foundations of Mysticism: Origins to the Fifth Century*, New York: Crossroad, 1991, p. xvii.

28. Main, *The Hunger for Depth and Meaning*, Kindle location 1756 of 2309.

29. Ibid., Kindle location 1679 of 2309.

30. Laurence Freeman writing in the foreword of *Our Hearts Burned within Us: Reading the New Testament with John Main*, Singapore: Medio Media, 2012, Kindle location 74 of 1185.

31. Bourgeault, *The Heart of Centering Prayer*, Kindle location 829 of 4494.

32. Laurence Freeman writing in the Foreword to Main, *Our Hearts Burned within Us: Reading the New Testament with John Main*, Kindle location 105 of 1185.

33. Julian of Norwich, *Showings*, 65. Quoted in Richard Rohr, *Daily Meditation*, 13 January 2015.

34. Main, *Word into Silence*, p. 4.

35. Laurence Freeman, *Health and Wholeness*, London: World Community for Christian Meditation, 2015, pp. 7–8.

36. 'A linear epistemology cannot accurately interpret a holographic way of knowing, and … there can be no phenomenology of the deep mind, because it is inaccessible to self-conscious mind except by intention.' Ross adds that '[The] highly metaphorical and internally filtered narratives [of such wisdom texts] have … often … been taken for literal descriptions of experience as opposed to being understood as textual experiences that point beyond themselves, engaging the reader in their process.' Maggie Ross, *Silence: A User's Guide (Volume 1: Process)*, London: Darton, Longman and Todd Ltd, 2014, pp. 25–6.

37. Ibid., pp. 47–8.

38. Ibid., Kindle location 410 of 5654.

39. Patrick Kavanagh, 'Having Confessed' in *Collected Poems*, W.W. Norton & Company, 2004, p. 149.

40. Ross, *Silence*, Kindle location 422 of 5654.

Chapter Three

Meditation and Children

Meditation with Children

Writing in the early 1990s about Christian meditation and children, Madeline Simon described children as 'born contemplatives', suggesting that children take to meditation 'like ducks to water' because 'they have not reached the stage of logical thought and are able, in their simplicity, to catch and hold God by love'.[1] John Main suggested that the opening of the human heart is as natural as the opening of a flower and many of the children experienced such heart-awareness when they sat in stillness and silence.[2] Because it is such a simple practice, it can be undertaken anywhere with minimal or no resources. It does not require advanced cognitive or technical ability to sit in silence. All it requires is the intention to simply be. There is no curriculum to follow. There are no books that children need to read before they can master it. Equally, it is non-competitive and there are no levels of achievement, no measuring stick to test proficiency, no weekly test. It is within the capacity of every child to meditate and all children can do it equally well.

The evidence is clear that children like to meditate. As the practice of meditation in a secular context has spread around the globe, frequently under the banner of 'mindfulness', it has also been introduced to young people and children. It is also growing as a spiritual practice in schools. A programme promoting Christian meditation with children is now active in twenty-six countries across the globe.[3] There are currently one hundred and fifty primary schools in Ireland engaged in the practice of meditation with children, generally twice each week, on a whole-school basis.[4] Many of the children also practise meditation at home. Alice (7), for example, meditated four times a day: 'When I wake up, in school, when I come home from school and before I go to bed – oh, and after swimming on Mondays.' Many of those who participated in the research eagerly practised meditation at home, some even teaching their parents how to meditate and meditating with them. We noted in chapter one that as a rule of thumb, children are encouraged to meditate for one minute per year of age – so a ten-year-old can meditate for ten minutes, and so on – however, children often begin with a shorter period and build up their practice over time. It is important to stress that meditation is a very ordinary experience for children, not something extraordinary. Once they have become used to the practice, its simplicity takes over and they just allow themselves to be. As Nuala (7) describes it, 'When I meditate I just ignore everything. When thoughts come into my mind, I just imagine wiping my head and they all go away.'

This chapter and the next contain many quotes directly from the children who participated in my doctoral research, which involved seventy children across four schools. The interview format was designed to allow space for the children to generate their own narratives and develop their ideas. I was particularly keen to try to enter into the mystery of the child's experience of the practice, especially to explore the extent to which the practice impacted, if at all, on their spirituality and the nature of that impact. As Rebecca Nye points out, when interviewing children about their spirituality, 'Non-verbal spiritual expressions and responses are very important, not just for younger, less verbal children, but also for those with fluent enough language.'[5] It is not simply a matter of asking appropriate, child-friendly questions and developing and using innovative methods, but about being fully present with and attentive to the child, attending to their feelings as much as, if not more than, the content of what they say and, also, being responsive to their non-verbal language throughout the interview. One must really listen to what children have to say.[6] This advice applies not just to researchers but also to parents and teachers as well.

I used simple questions such as 'If meditation was a colour, what colour would it be?' This approach allowed children to move beyond conceptual thinking and to tap into perceptual knowledge. I used photo-elicitation for the same reason. The children were invited to look at a selection of thirty A4-sized photographs depicting a range of life experiences and to choose three or four that most reminded them of their experience of meditation.[7] They were then invited to describe what they saw in each chosen image before exploring why it reminded them of meditation.[8] This approach worked well, enabling the children to give metaphorical expression to their inner world; for example, one child compared meditation to a mother feeding her baby.

Following the first round of interviews in each school, a range of emerging common responses was identified, and from this a set of comment cards, each holding a brief statement such as 'meditation calms me' or 'meditation awakens my heart', was developed. These cards were presented to each child in their second interview and they were asked if each statement meant anything to them. They then placed any card that resonated into a 'selection box' and were asked to describe what it meant to them in terms of their experience of meditation. This approach helped children to comment on things that other children had said; ideas that carried meaning for them but that they had not mentioned themselves in their own first interview.

What It Can Be Like for a Child to Meditate

What is it like for a child to experience meditation? How do children describe that which they encounter in the silence? I now present an account of what it can be like for a child to experience meditation, based on the children's accounts.[9] I want to enter an important caveat here. This is not the experience of any one child; nor is it intended to suggest that any child will experience all of the elements included in the description. Although written in the first person, the description is a composite of the comments of many different children.[10] Its purpose is to give the reader a strong sense of what the experience can be like, a rich sense of how meditation can be experienced. It provides a form of access to the experience that, on the one hand, is not directly sayable, but yet uses words that somehow make it knowable and understandable, so that the reader gets a sense of the potential richness of the experience.[11] Because it is written in the first person, a composite narrative like this may give the impression that the experience is more dramatically powerful than it is; that is not the intention. Instead, it is included because some aspect or other of the description may resonate with the reader and convey to the reader a deeper understanding of what it can be like for a child to meditate. As far as possible, the description that follows uses actual phrases and idioms as employed by the children themselves, interwoven with some imaginative description based on the researcher's knowledge and personal experience.[12]

A Description of the Child's Experience of Meditation

I like meditation because it's so peaceful and quiet. Especially in school, because everyone is really quiet at the same time. When it started first I thought it would be boring. I didn't think I would be able to do it. But I can and I really like it now. If meditation was a colour it would be yellow, because when I see the colour yellow I am all of a sudden so happy. Meditation makes me happy too.

Meditation gives you a break from your worries. Sometimes you don't know you need a break until you take it and then it feels so good when you do. I discovered that for myself. It's not like you're asleep or anything, but it's a different kind of being awake. I saw a beautiful picture of fish swimming in a coral reef and it reminded me of meditation. Everything was bright and colourful and the fish were happy and free. They could just be themselves. It made me realise that meditation is like that for me. I can just be myself.

Meditation brings me inside myself. It feels like it is somewhere deep inside. I can't describe the feeling. I can't compare it to anything else. It feels like you are just thinking – well, not thinking, but just sitting there. I'm not thinking about what's going to happen next. It's like I'm in a bubble. It feels like there is nothing around me and I feel like I'm in freedom. Meditation is like walking along a path curving into a wood; you don't know what's in there but you want to go in and you know it will be safe.

When I meditate it feels like my whole body has stopped. I've stopped moving, I've stopped working and I just feel at peace with the world. A certain kind of emotion comes inside of me and it makes me feel better. It makes me feel happier in the world and it makes me feel grateful for everything good in my life. If I was in bad form before meditation, I feel good afterwards. I don't know why, but whatever was bothering me doesn't seem to matter so much after meditation. I'm able to let it go.

Even when it's noisy outside, it doesn't feel noisy inside me – it feels calm and quiet. Whatever is happening around me doesn't disturb that. I can hear the sounds around – the rain on the roof, cars passing by, a dog barking – but I let it all go. It's like I'm slowly sinking into myself and, when I get deep enough, it's as if my heart opens up and I realise more what I'm feeling. I'm not thinking about my feelings, but I feel them more. I realise how I actually feel and how others feel. Sometimes I realise that something I said or did at lunchtime wasn't nice and that I need to apologise for it. Then I'm able to let it go and after meditation I say sorry.

Some days after meditation I get the same feeling I would have if I had something really special and exciting to look forward to. It makes me want to get back into the day so it can happen. Meditation gives me energy. I'm more focused afterwards. It's like all the stuff that had built up in the morning is gone and there's loads of space for starting again.

Wherever I am when I meditate, it feels like I'm just here now and this is exactly where I'm supposed to be. Even when I'm meditating at school, the feeling of being in school completely goes out of my mind. It brings me to a place of joy and happiness and it feels like I'm somewhere I always wanted to be since I was small. It feels like everything is right with the world. I'm not thinking about happy things, but it's as if I'm surrounded by happiness. My heart feels really happy. It's as if the space that is filled when all my thoughts and worries have left … it's as if that space is filled by happiness and love.

But some days meditation makes me happy and sad at the same time. My nana died last year and I always feel she is close to me in meditation. That makes me a little bit sad because I miss her but happy at the same time because I feel close to her when I meditate and I feel that she is close to me and that she loves me. I always feel different after meditation. Meditation makes me feel safe and loved.

After meditation, I feel like I'm a better person. Meditation makes me realise all the goodness inside me and in everybody. Even people I don't really like or who are not very nice to me. Even bad people, only they can't see it. It's as if I've reached a certain part of me that has most of the goodness and once you meditate you can kind of figure out where it is and let it show. It feels like this is who I really am. And, often, it feels like God is there, filling my heart with love. I feel loved by my family and loved by God. I don't worry about what's going to happen next. I just let everything be itself. And me be me.

Four key motifs emerged from the children's descriptions, which together capture the essence of what it feels like to meditate as a child: simplicity, serenity, self-awareness and heart-awareness.[13]

Firstly, it was evident that the children found the practice of meditation came easily to them. There was nothing to be achieved – the aim was simply to be. The children had no sense of 'having to do it'. Although the children recognised it was simple, that didn't mean it was *always* easy. A number of children spoke of the struggle it presented some days. Frank (9) noticed that while he usually relaxes in meditation, there were times when instead he becomes tight and stiff. When asked what made the difference he replied, 'I think it's better if you don't concentrate too hard, don't try too hard, just say your word and it just works. It's easier if you don't think you are doing meditation, you're *not doing* anything.' Paul (9) chose the image of a dejected-looking rag doll as an image that reminded him of meditation, 'He's real annoyed. He looks angry or annoyed and he needs to meditate, but it looks like he's just tried meditating and it doesn't work.' Tara (11) observed that sometimes in meditation she becomes aware of an itch and she finds it very difficult to refrain from scratching it. But when she ignores it, she realises when the meditation is finished that the itch is no longer there. It really didn't need to be scratched!

The children in this study seemed to have a childlike understanding that the secret to meditation is effortless intention. Many adults struggle with this, probably because they have accumulated so much conceptual baggage. They are not comfortable with not-knowing. Some adults seem to experience a compulsion to figure it out fully before they are willing to cross over the threshold. But it cannot be figured out conceptually. Ultimately, meditation gives rise to perceptual, not conceptual knowledge.

Secondly, the children found their meditation sessions to be very serene, calming and relaxing. As we noted in chapter one, Leanne (9) described meditation as 'a break from all the drama'. The children loved the peace and quiet that it generated. Weronika (7) observed, 'My body feels slower and rested, soft and relaxed.' Molly (10) related meditation to an image of a bird sitting on a branch:

> He's just sitting on a branch, he doesn't have any worries. Birds don't really have any worries. They don't know what's going to happen to them next and they don't mind. They just go along with life.

Lucy (10) chose an image of three ballerina-like figures floating against a blue background:

> What I like about this picture is that when you're doing meditation, it's like all of the anger is flying out of you. Because if you're angry it's as if it is 'staked' into you but when you do meditation it's just like it all flies away.

Many children referred, in one way or another, to a sense of being ever more present to themselves and to developing a rich sense of their deepest potential. The very practice of sitting in silence made them keenly aware of their thoughts, emotions and feelings, even as they let them go and returned to saying their sacred word. As well as developing a sense of self-awareness, the children also found that they discovered a capacity to stand back from the thoughts, feelings and emotions that arose. They found they were no longer imprisoned by them. Grace (9) described it as follows, 'Meditation helps me to figure it out and to feel it more and to be more of what I'm feeling and not to just hide it ... Meditation helps me to be free and not to be trapped in my feelings. If I'm feeling sad inside, I just decide I'm going to let it go.' In the longer term, their awareness of their inner reality helped to transform their way of seeing the world, especially when they found themselves in danger of becoming overwhelmed by circumstances. In addition, many children found that after meditation, solutions to problems sometimes presented themselves out of the blue. For example, Aideen (11) discovered that, sometimes after meditation she would realise that, 'I had figured out something that I didn't even know I was thinking about ... but, the thinking must have been going on the whole time.' While she used the word 'thinking', it seems clear she meant that the problem was somehow being processed at a level of consciousness deeper than her ordinary, everyday self-consciousness. Linked to this awareness of presence to self, a recurring theme across all of the children related to a sense of inner spaciousness. For many of the children this experience of spaciousness was linked to a sense of freedom, the freedom to be themselves. As Pamela (11) expressed it, 'You kind of go into your own world and you have a sense that everything is okay; it feels like a good place to be and you realise that it's fine to be totally yourself.'

And, finally, many children also sensed a connection to something greater than themselves, a sense of relationship with that which transcended their everyday sense of themselves. They hinted at intimations of divine presence and a sense of connection with others and all of creation. Because many religious traditions describe the spiritual centre as the 'heart', I named this experience 'heart-awareness' and it points, I believe, towards a growing awareness of their true essence, their true-self. Many children spoke spontaneously about a sense of divine presence in meditation, often using the familiar expression 'God' to verbalise it. Leanne (9) described how she physically experienced God's presence, 'I feel it in my heart. I just feel like my heart is knocking. No, not knocking; it just warms up when I meditate.' Grace (9) considered that God 'is actually very, very close to us, when everyone thinks he's really faraway'. Adrian (11) simply, and remarkably, said he considered God was both very close and far away at the same time, 'I think, God has the power to be at one with everyone at the same time.' While Norah (10) said that she felt close to God when she meditates in her room:

> I get my communion candle and I light it and I feel like he's there in the flame. He is there watching me as I meditate. I sense that through the freedom I feel.

She went on to say that when they meditate in school it's as if each person is a lit candle and God 'flies into each candle, leaving hope in each one'.

The Spirituality of Children

To describe the basic human desire for insight into the meaning of life, Kees Waaijman uses the expression 'primordial spirituality', 'because this type of spirituality belongs to the basic processes of human existence ... beyond or prior to the type of spirituality as it is institutionalised' in the religions of the world.[14] In other words, spirituality may be considered as an inner drive to live an authentic life, a drive that finds expression in all religious traditions – theistic and non-theistic – and none. This dynamic, this drive can be described in secular terms or in terms of a particular faith or religious tradition. Spirituality, then, is a natural, innate human predisposition. Yet, despite the growing awareness of the innate spiritual capacity of the human person, it was not until the late 1970s that scholars and others began to consider spiritual awareness as a universal human attribute accessible by children.[15] It is now widely accepted that children do have an innate capacity for spirituality, even if they lack the ability to adequately verbalise their spiritual experience. Karl Rahner's view that human persons, including children, are innately oriented toward God provides support for this consensus. For Rahner, it is the child's capacity for 'infinite openness' that enlivens their spirituality, which arises from within, from their own existence and experience.[16]

It is difficult to find a precise definition for spirituality because, like beauty, it is an abstract concept. Many people have focused instead on describing the characteristics of children's spirituality. Nye identified a common core characteristic in the accounts of the children she interviewed about their spiritual experience, which she named 'relational consciousness'.[17] In other words, children have an innate capacity for relationship, which is the foundation of their relationship with themselves, with others, with all of creation and with God. Other characteristics include a capacity for joy, wonder and awe and the gift of imaginative wondering. Spirituality also manifests in children in terms of their search for identity, meaning and purpose. Children's spirituality has an everyday rather than a dramatic quality about it. While children give free expression to the characteristics just described, their engagement with it seems to diminish as they approach their teenage years. Hay and Nye suggest that in the modern secular world the innate spirituality of children is 'being obscured, overlaid or even repressed by socially constructed processes' that contradict it; in other words, the culture of modern society is, in many respects, not just indifferent but hostile to the public expression of spirituality.[18] My own research suggests that meditation has the capacity to counter this tendency.

We saw in the last chapter that the understanding of spirituality underpinning my research on meditation with children is related to the concept of the true-self. Thomas Merton saw the discovery of the true-self as an experience of finding God deep within the centre of the human person. When we experience this form of conscious awareness, it is not merely psychological insight but an experiential insight into our participating in Being itself. In this state of consciousness, we no longer perceive ourselves as objects but as participants in Being. This is perceptual, spiritual knowledge and most adults, let alone children, would have difficulty expressing it in words. Nonetheless, in the silence and stillness of meditation many children experience a sense of spaciousness within, which is ultimately inseparable from Being. In Christian terms, children's spirituality may be understood, then, as that deep, albeit obscure, inner awareness of one's true essence, of the true-self, of the reality that we are all beloved children of God.

Meditation and Spiritual Experience in Children

We have seen how Ken Wilber came to see human development as a progressive movement through stages of human consciousness. Both he and Allan Combs learned to distinguish between the stages of human consciousness and states of human consciousness. We are all familiar with the three main states of consciousness, which are waking, dreaming, and deep sleep.[19] In addition, meditation can give rise to altered states of consciousness.[20] As one continues with the regular practice of meditation, one's awareness of ever subtler states of consciousness begins to unfold. Such awareness is perceptual, not conceptual, and is impossible to describe in words.[21] Perhaps the easiest way to apprehend this is to attempt to recall a peak experience you had in the past, such as when you became totally lost in a beautiful sunset – perhaps so much so that nothing distinguished you from it. Tobin Hart tells the story of eight-year-old Miranda, who spent an hour in the sea, with the water up to her waist, 'swaying in the surf in the same spot' and who announced when she came out, 'It was amazing. I was the water. I love it and it loves me. I don't know how else to say it.'[22]

Children are too young to understand very much about life. In their simplicity, they are comfortable with the limited and emergent nature of their knowledge, with not-knowing; they know they have so much to learn about the world. Because of this they remain open to possibility. They have a trust in their innate way of knowing, in their perceptual knowledge. By comparison, as we grow into adulthood and our capacity for conceptual knowledge enlarges we begin to doubt the validity and value of perceptual knowledge. As we become more rational, we tend to think that everything can be explained in words and concepts and we tend to distrust perceptual knowledge. While adults generally feel the need to analyse, to explain and to control their environment, children are open to allowing life to unfold its mysteries. Whereas adults are often deeply uncomfortable with anything that cannot be expressed clearly in words, children seem to embody the understanding that while knowledge may be complex, wisdom is simple. They are able to leave themselves open to whatever may transpire in the silence, without having to understand it or explain it.

The key point to grasp here is that the Wilber and Combs distinction between stages and states helps to explain how it is that children can access very deep states of spiritual consciousness, even with limited cognitive development. While their growth through the stages of consciousness depends on their age, life experience and education, they can encounter temporary deep states of consciousness at any age and any stage. Stages can only be experienced like steps on a ladder, one after the other. Generally speaking, each stage is a permanent acquisition – one rarely loses the capacities that accompany it. But states work differently; one can experience a very deep spiritual state but it will be a temporary experience. Unlike stages, states never become a permanent acquisition. Meditation gives rise to such temporary states. During meditation, in the gap between thoughts, one's state of consciousness is briefly altered and deepened, even though the self-conscious mind will not be aware of it at the time. This happens over and over again in every meditation session. As we develop a habit of meditating regularly, we repeatedly access deeper states of consciousness and it becomes easier to access that state of consciousness more readily, just as exercising a particular muscle or set of muscles strengthens one's capacity to use it beneficially with ever greater ease.

The insight of Wilber and Combs helps us to understand that while children may access deeply spiritual experiences through the practice of meditation, their capacity to give expression to that experience will be limited by their age and their general stage of consciousness (including their cognitive and language development as children). If they attempt to describe their spiritual experience, their verbal expression will be childlike, appropriate to their age. It may be interpreted by adults as irrational although it may, in fact, be trans-rational, beyond the capacity of words or concepts to describe. Parents and teachers need to understand this, otherwise they may all too readily dismiss what their children say and contribute inadvertently to the suppression of their child's innate spirituality. Bearing this in mind, in the next chapter we will explore what children themselves have to say as they describe their experience of the fruits of meditation.

Practice Four

Now that you have a better understanding of what it means to meditate, why not set the timer on your phone for ten minutes and enjoy a ten-minute meditation.

Follow the instructions in practice two (page 62) but this time extend your period of meditation to ten minutes.

Endnotes

1. Madeleine Simon, *Born Contemplative: Introducing Children to Christian Meditation*, London: Darton, Longman and Todd, 1993, p. 2.

2. John Main, *Community of Love*, Singapore: Medio Media, 2010, Kindle location 1594 of 2952.

3. The practice is being promoted by the World Community for Christian Meditation. For further detail, see Jim Green, *The Heart of Education: Meditation with Children and Young People*, London: Meditatio – World Community for Christian Meditation, 2016.

4. The practice has been introduced to over thirty-five thousand children in those schools.

5. Rebecca Nye, *Children's Spirituality: What It Is and Why It Matters*, London: Church House Publishing, 2009, p. 27.

6. David Hay and Rebecca Nye, *The Spirit of the Child*, revised edn, London: Jessica Kingsley Publishers, 1998, p. 64.

7. The photographs included, for example, images of adults and children in happy and unhappy settings, scenes of nature in beautiful and polluted settings, as well as a range of abstract images. No image was chosen in the hope it would generate a particular response – rather, the images were chosen to represent a diversity of everyday lived experience.

8. A selection of the photographs, each originally A4 in size, are available online at www.christianmeditation.ie

9. Within the field of phenomenological research the description is referred to technically as a phenomenological description.

10. For further information on the use of composite first-person narrative see Les Todres, *Embodied Enquiry: Phenomenological Touchstones for Research, Psychotherapy and Spirituality*, Basingstoke, UK: Palgrave Macmillan, 2007, p. 50.

11. A phenomenological description mediates one's intuitive grasp of the experience or aspects of it. See Max van Manen, *Phenomonology of Practice: Meaning-Giving Methods in Phenomenological Research and Writing*, Walnut Creek, CA: Left Coast Press, Inc., 2014, Kindle location 6450 of 11092.

12. Van Manen notes, 'An anecdote can be constructed from "lived experience descriptions" gathered through interview, observation, personal experience, related literature, written accounts, or from imagined accounts. Sometimes experiential descriptions are so well

narrated that they already have the narrative shape of an anecdote.'
Ibid., Kindle location 6222 of 11092.

13. Rather appropriately, these motifs might be summarised by the interjection 'Sssh!' This is particularly apt because meditation is the disciplined practice of silence.

14. Kees Waaijman, 'Challenges of Spirituality in Contemporary Times' in *Spirituality Forum III*, University of Santo Tomas, Manila, Philippines, 2003, p. 1, www.isa.org.ph/pdf/Waaijman.pdf, accessed 4 December 2014.

15. See, for example, Sofia Cavalletti, *The Religious Potential of the Child: The Description of an Experience with Children from Ages Three to Six*, The Missionary Society of St Paul the Apostle (trans.), New York: Paulist Press, 1983; Tobin Hart, *The Secret Spiritual World of Children*, Novato, CA: New World Library, 2003; Robert Coles, *The Spiritual Life of Children*, London: HarperCollins, 1992; Joanne Taylor, *Inner Wisdom: Children as Spiritual Guides*, New York: Pilgrim Press, 1989.

16. Mary Ann Hinsdale, '"Infinite Openness to the Infinite": Karl Rahner's Contribution to Modern Catholic Thought on the Child' in *The Child in Christian Thought*, Marcia J. Bunge (ed.), Grand Rapids, Michigan: Wm. B. Eerdmans Publishing Co., 2001.

17. Hay and Nye, *The Spirit of the Child*. See also Nye, *Children's Spirituality*.

18. Hay and Nye, *The Spirit of the Child*, p. 140.

19. Our knowledge of deep sleep comes mostly from those who have studied it as we do not seem to self-consciously experience deep sleep.

20. As we observed earlier, such states of consciousness may lie beyond self-consciousness, as deep sleep generally does; but we can be aware we have experienced them by the traces they leave behind and by our growth in perceptual knowledge. There are also other altered states of consciousness such as trance states, hypnotic states and alcohol or drug-induced states.

21. Many meditative traditions hold that 'meditation trains the capacity of systematic apperception of the structures of individual, subjective consciousness toward apprehension of consciousness in pure subjectivity, or consciousness itself.' See Olga Louchakova-Schwartz, 'Cognitive Phenomenology in the Study of Tibetan Meditation: Phenomenological Descriptions Versus Meditation Styles' in Susan Gordan (ed.), *Neurophenomenology and Its Applications to Psychology*, New York: Springer Science and Business Media, 2013, p. 68.

22. Hart, *The Secret Spiritual World of Children*, p. 47.

Chapter Four

What Children Say about the Fruits of Meditation

In addition to the benefits of meditation, the wisdom traditions have long asserted that the practice also has the capacity to produce deep spiritual fruits. So, does meditation have the capacity to produce such fruits in children and, if so, how do they experience those fruits in their lives? Ernie Christie suggests that it leads to increased self-knowledge and self-acceptance in children and deepens their personal relationship with God.[1] In this chapter, I set out, in the children's own words, how they experienced the fruits of meditation in their lives.

How Children Describe the Fruits of Meditation

The four fruits as expressed by the children in their conversations with me were: meditation helps you to be yourself; helps you to feel the goodness inside; brings you closer to God; makes you a kinder person.

~ You Can Be Yourself
~ You Feel the Goodness Deep Inside
~ You Become Closer to God
~ You Become a Kinder Person

Figure 4.1 How Children Describe the Fruits of Meditation

Meditation Helps You to Be Yourself

The children observed that meditation made them more aware of what is happening within and helped them to be themselves. Grace (9) said she learned through meditation, 'When I'm not being myself, I'm not being honest.' Kate (11) said that one of the reasons she would tell someone to meditate is 'to figure out who you really are and to accept who you are'. Jack (11) observed, 'Sometimes when I'm angry or upset, I don't feel like I'm the real me. But then I meditate and I find that I am the real me.' Norah (10) said meditation made her realise, 'I'm this person. I'm not any other person. When I meditate I feel more "me" than I ever did before.' Pamela (11), having chosen the image of a bird on a branch as one that reminded her of meditation, commented, 'I see a bird looking into the sky and thinking "Why don't I go out there and show them who I really am"'. Elsewhere in her conversation, she observed:

> I think meditation brings out the real me, and I don't have to pretend to be someone else. I used to want to be like the cool kids in my class, instead of being me. I wanted to be as pretty as them, to behave like them. But when I meditate, I can be myself and I accept myself for who I am. I can't change anything and I accept that I'm me. I realise it's just really nice to be myself.

These conversations, which gave voice to the children's sense of their deepest nature, their true-self, were laced with tensions around fitting in and peer pressure. David (10) spoke of the tension of wanting to fit in with the 'gang' and how meditation gave him the courage to be himself:

> I think meditation helps me to be myself, to accept myself as I am. Most people try and fit in, to be with a gang of lads who are really popular. They might not like them, but they want to be with them because they are so popular. But they should learn to be themselves, and to be with friends that they actually like.

Meditation seems to engender a capacity for detachment: children begin to notice how their preoccupations and conditioning imprison them and they discover that this awareness is often enough to free them from their attachments. This enables them to be true to themselves, to respond as they really want to rather than act according to how they think others expect them to. Leanne (9) observed, 'If I'm fighting with my brother and I meditate, I get freedom from being caught up in that situation. I'm able to move on.' And Norah (10) reported, 'When I'm worried or stressed, it weighs me down, as if there are heavy chains around my neck. But when I meditate, I feel like they just fall away and I'm just like [sounding a sigh of relief] I'm just free.' Lena (11) used a similar metaphor, observing that 'When your mind is full of worries and troubles, it's like you are locked in a cage but then when you meditate, you begin to feel free; you are able to picture your own path and you follow it.'

Many children spoke of this deepening sense of inner freedom and realising there was a deep well of wisdom within themselves that meditation helped them to draw from. Julia (12) felt that meditation brought her deeper inside herself:

> You are not talking when you're meditating, so it takes you more inside. I usually keep my thoughts and feelings inside me … but after meditation I will sometimes start talking about what I feel, because I feel so relaxed after it. It makes me much more flexible.

Jason (12) described the capacity for being more attentive as a matter of noticing his behaviour more, 'Before I meditated, I didn't really care about how I behaved, but now I'm starting to notice it. And I'm starting to get a handle on it.' Adrian (11) too noticed that he was becoming more sensitive and responsive to the needs of others. He said this happens because in meditation, 'I shut off my brain and I open up my heart. When my heart is open I "get" other people's feelings more'. Many children noted that meditation gave them a better perspective on things. What seemed like a big problem before meditation doesn't bother them at all after meditation. For example, Sophie (8) commented, 'Say if your friends were being mean to you, meditation makes you realise that maybe they were just cross or angry for some reason.' Helena (7) found that meditation made her more sensitive to the feelings of others:

> When meditation is deep in you, you feel like you are somewhere you've always wanted to be since you were small. And you can actually think about what you actually feel like and how others feel. And then if you're

not happy with someone you can say sorry. You realise 'I did something wrong' and then you go and say sorry. And afterwards you'll feel happy again.

These examples demonstrate that the children experience meditation as helping them to become more aware of themselves and to be true to who they really are. The regular practice of meditation seems to increase children's capacity to see themselves non-judgementally and non-dualistically and to see others as other selves, not merely as objects.

Meditation Helps You to Feel the Goodness Deep Inside

Very many children spoke of becoming intensely aware in meditation of their own inherent goodness and feeling a strong sense that they are unconditionally loved. For example, Jack (11) said, 'When I'm angry I don't feel the goodness inside, but when I meditate, then I do feel the goodness in me.' And Sophie (8) noted, 'Meditation helps me to be more aware of the goodness inside me.' Lucy (10) described that, 'When you're not doing meditation, you sort of ... have a snap inside you. As if you are always getting ready to snap. But when you do meditation, the goodness comes out. The bad feelings disappear and the goodness flows in.' Derek (9) felt that meditation 'releases kindness in you ... and makes you feel more open-minded.' Barry (10) expressed the same idea a little differently, saying that sometimes people act badly, forgetting they are really good on the inside and 'meditation helps me to understand that if someone is behaving badly, that there is still goodness inside of them. And I think if they meditated they might realise that for themselves.' In other words, as well as making them aware of the goodness within themselves, meditation also helped children to become more keenly aware of the innate goodness in others.

It seems that many children recognise that the goodness deep inside themselves and others is who they really are. The practice of meditation seems to create an opportunity for self-recognition at a very deep level, which makes children keenly aware of the tension that arises within when they do not live up to this innate goodness, when their thoughts or actions are in conflict with their sense of their true-self. It helps the children to deal with unkind comments from others. Derek (9) commented that if someone says something nasty to him it can make him feel bad inside 'but when I do meditation I feel different. Something inhabits inside of me that makes me feel I am still a good person. When I meditate it helps me feel that, whatever anyone says, I know this is who I am.' And it is that understanding, rather than the initial hurt, that determines his response. Those who see goodness in the other naturally draw forth the good in people, leading to better relationships all round.

This sense of their innate goodness was experienced as heart-centred. Aimee said that meditation felt really good and, placing a hand on her heart, indicated that she felt warmth around her heart when she meditated. Lucy (10), referring to her sense that meditation brought her deeper inside herself, observed that normally 'you don't pay attention to your heart. But when you're in meditation, you don't use your brain.

Instead, you are realising what's inside you – what you are inside. And you are your heart'. Jason (12) said that the energy he gets from meditation 'comes from the heart … as if your heart is telling you a good thing'. In these comments Lucy and Jason capture, in their own way, the subtle distinction between conceptual and perceptual knowledge. Lucy is suggesting that in meditation, she does not engage in conceptual thinking but she is aware that (perceptual) knowledge, nonetheless, arises in her consciousness – her feelings surface and make themselves more intimately known in a way that might be described as primordial or perceptual, as knowledge that presents itself to the conscious mind which is not the result of thoughtful reflection.[2] I noted earlier that Aideen (11) referred to this too, describing perceptual knowledge as 'thinking subconsciously'. Doireann (11) also hints at this process of perceptual discovery, in her own unique way:

> When you meditate you discover things you didn't know. It's like a secret garden that you don't find, even though you walk by it every day. And then, suddenly, you discover it. It's just a hidden part of you that no one knows about, not even yourself. But one day you just come across it and you keep it to yourself. You don't really tell anyone about it … It fills everything with love and hope. But it's hard to explain.

For children the goodness within, their essential nature, is experienced as heart-centred. Many noted that meditation made them feel a deep sense of gratitude.

Meditation Brings You Closer to God

Children experience, as they meditated, a sense of being surrounded by happiness and love. One of the motifs of their meditation experience was described as heart-awareness and it captured their fleeting sense of connection to something greater than themselves. With regular practice, that sense of connection deepened and many children described meditation as bringing them closer to God. In other words, meditation enkindled and nurtured their innate spirituality. Natalie (11) expressed this very succinctly:

> Meditation helps me to connect with God because normally we are so busy and we don't pay attention to God. But when we meditate, we get about five or ten minutes to connect with God and to feel closer. I take a few minutes, not to talk to him, but to be with him, to feel closer to him.

Ella (9) noted, 'When I meditate it feels like me and God are connected. It feels like he's giving me loads of love when I'm meditating. I can feel his love. And sometimes in my sleep, in my dreams, I'm meditating and I can see God sitting there beside me meditating.' We saw earlier that Norah (10) described feeling really close to God in meditation. Although she located his presence in the flame of her communion candle, her body language made it clear that she experienced his presence in her heart. Aideen (11), too, said, 'I think we can all be like God if we try, so … we all have a little bit of God in us.' Nessa (11) described her sense of being connected to God somewhat differently. She explained that meditation made her feel that she was deeply loved and that she 'knows' God. Emelia (9) considered God and meditation to be intimately connected; for her, 'Meditation feels exciting, like goodness is flowing through me.'

Many children liked the fact that the whole school meditated together because it made for one big happy family. For example, Adrian (11) felt his sense of being connected to God in meditation was strengthened by the fact that the whole school meditated together, saying:

> It feels like everyone is one. Everyone's eyes are closed. We're all together and still it feels like there is just no one. It feels like no one is around you, as if everyone is where you are now. And God is in the presence.

This is a profound statement for an eleven-year-old and suggests that meditation has the capacity to impact on the whole school community. Adrian was not alone; many of the children commented that meditation made them feel God's love not just for themselves but also for others. Barry (10) said:

> God is always beside you. And I think you feel love when God is close to you. He is everywhere you could say and, he shares love with everyone, not just you. So, you can feel closer to all of that.

Nessa (11) says that when she meditates she goes 'on a journey down to God. And then God just appears. He doesn't talk. It's just like a sense that he is there. And I can see my granddad [who passed away] in the background.' She was one of many children who linked their meditation with a sense of being very close to relatives who had passed from this life. As Ella (9) expressed it, 'It's like we can communicate when I'm meditating.'

Although these children are young, they are not entirely naive. As well as stating that they experienced a sense of God's presence in meditation, some of the children indicated that they struggled to come to terms with what that actually meant. Adrian (11) said he sometimes wondered if God was real but 'then when I get that feeling in meditation, it really makes me feel like God is real'. The sense of struggle described by Adrian is important and points to the implicit but unspoken distinction between conceptual and perceptual knowledge. This may point to an urgent need to speak with children about their experience of perceptual knowledge and how it can manifest itself in their lives in the context of their spiritual development and in their appreciation of poetry, drama and art. Children seem to apprehend intuitively that the landscape they are traversing as they meditate, the landscape of the heart, cannot adequately be understood or described because it is ineffable. It seems possible, perhaps likely, that for these children the practice of meditation provides an opportunity to experience over and over again that heartfelt sense of presence that transcends them, yet makes itself felt, however subtly. There is a sense of being touched by God, of being embraced so lightly and gently – a sense that was captured by Gráinne who liked to feel the breeze against her skin as she meditated near an open window because 'it's so light and God won't play rough, he'll just touch you very carefully'.

Aideen (11) spoke about an incident she had witnessed where a woman fell to the floor in a supermarket and was ignored by those nearest her. One man, however, moved quickly to help her. Aideen said that made her realise that some people don't enhance their inner God, and some people, like the man who helped, do: 'They enhance their inner God and let it shine through.' She went on to say, 'I use the meditation time to let my inner God show. I would hope that if someone had problems, say like a criminal who got into trouble, I would hope that meditation would help them to change their lifestyle and let their inner God show and not be back and forth from prison all the time.'

Derek (9) described his sense of being connected to God in meditation in terms of being nourished and energised by that connection:

> When I meditate I feel as if I have called to God. I feel as if I'm asking God to come closer to me, to help me to do other things. And I feel there is something like … a certain stretching of me. It gives me the ability to concentrate, to feel more aware and think before I do something … I feel like God is telling me something.

Karen (7) spoke of this inner nourishment when she chose an image of a red rose as one that reminded her of meditation. In the picture, the rose is sprinkled with drops of water, as if after a spring shower. She commented, 'It reminds me of meditation because God let the flower have some water so it has room to grow.' Kate (11) too used the image of the red rose to describe very beautifully her understanding that meditation nourished her spirit:

> This flower just got watered so it's growing. Like our soul is growing every day. It's growing stronger. As you can see, before it was just this small little thing and now it has opened out ... We are all beautiful on the inside. And that beauty will shine. This image is saying 'This is the world and this is who I am. And I'm going to let my spirit grow.'

Kate (11) chose the image of a blue bird sitting still on a branch as one that reminded her of meditation:

> I chose this image because the bird is sitting still and I am still in meditation. I see a tree, a living tree, like a living person. And the bird, like the brain is peaceful and still; nothing is bothering it and everything is calm. The buds on the tree are about to blossom – it's as if its spirit is blossoming.

This is a very rich metaphor and Kate went on to say that meditation helped her spirit to blossom, 'It's like it says to you, "Okay, now it's your time to grow."' And Pamela (11) described meditation as like a mother feeding her baby, but, she added, 'your spirit is the baby ... And God is the mother.'

All of these excerpts point to the fact that these children experienced a strong heartfelt sense of inner, spiritual nourishment as a fruit of the practice of meditation. While they found it difficult to give voice to it explicitly in words, they did so beautifully through metaphors. Their remarkable use of metaphor suggests that they had come to know perceptually truths that are beyond conceptual knowledge and captured their sense of an intimate, almost inexpressible, connection with the transcendent. These accounts suggest that meditation helps children to begin to trust in that perceptual knowledge, to appropriate its deepest meanings at a non-conceptual level, deepening their own sense of being connected to God.

Meditation Makes You a Kinder Person

As well as nourishing their spirituality – helping them to discover their true-self, who they really are in God – many also spoke of how they experienced meditation as a form of guidance, nudging them in the direction of acting responsibly and doing the right thing. Sophie (8) found meditation made her a kinder person: 'When I let go of the things that are bothering me, it's like I've become a kinder person. If I've done unkind things to others, it makes me realise that's not who I am. It makes me kinder and I go and say sorry.' Jason (12) described his sense that meditation was 'pushing me in the direction of my inner person, towards what I should be. Meditation feeds you in a spiritual way. And knowledge-wise as well. Because it helps you to think about the person you should be.'

Meditation with Children

Meditation seemed to give the children access to an inner wisdom, an inner truth and they allow themselves to be guided by it. This suggests they were able to access an inner dynamism that guided them towards more authentic living, towards more meaningful relationship with themselves, others and God. Aideen (11) described this innate drive as her 'inner eye', a concept she had learned from Wordworth's poem 'I Wandered Lonely as a Cloud'. Grace (9) described it in terms of honesty, 'Meditation helps you be honest with yourself and be honest with your friends and everyone around you, because if you're not honest with yourself, you can't be honest with anyone else. When I'm talking to God I can be honest, the most honest I want to be. I don't have to pretend or hide anything from anyone when I'm in meditation.'

The subtle language of the children reveals how meditation seems to lead them to a kind of insightful knowledge, which seems to come from nowhere but which they attribute to the practice of meditation. It is not that they have come to a conclusion having carefully considered the pros and cons of a situation and worked out what is best for them when faced with a challenge or a dilemma. Instead, it is as if they are inspired to respond rather than react; as if, somehow, deep within the psyche, they have come to understand what response the particular situation calls for and they are inspired to act on it. Although it may seem paradoxical, it seems that the practice of self-forgetfulness leads to a growing sense of self-responsibility and the capacity to act on it.

From the examples quoted in this section it is clear that the children did not merely experience spiritual nourishment as a fruit of meditation but it went on to impact their daily lives.

~ You Can Be Yourself
~ You Feel the Goodness Deep Inside
~ You Become Closer to God
~ You Become a Kinder Person

Fruits

~ Deepens Self-Awareness
~ Awakens the Heart to the True-Self
~ Nourishes the Spirit
~ Inspires Authentic Living

Fruits

Figure 4.2 The Fruits of Meditation Renamed

Meditation somehow guided them to make better decisions, made them kinder and more appreciative of the point of view of others and inspired them to be the best person they could be. This can be interpreted as a deep desire to live out the values of the true-self, which they discerned deep within themselves, however obscurely. So far, the fruits of meditation for children have been described in the children's own words, as shown in the upper panel of Figure 4.2. The lower panel expresses the same fruits in more formal language: meditation deepens their self-awareness; awakens the heart to the true-self within; nourishes their spirituality and inspires them towards authentic, compassionate living. These four fruits are also represented graphically in Figure 4.3.

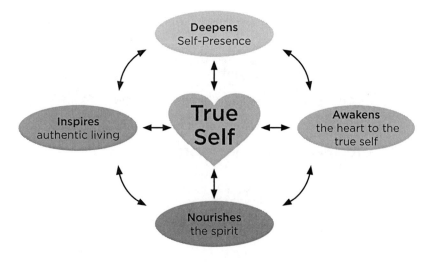

Figure 4.3 Graphic Depiction of the Fruits of Meditation

Employing a very rich metaphor, Jason (12) said he saw meditation as a map:

> Meditation pulls you ... *Meditation is like a map and the destination is who you really are* and it's pointing you in directions ... it's pointing you towards ... the destination is your inner person and it makes you want to be a better person than what you, like how you act now ... It's pulling your towards ... it's like it's pulling me towards ... to be a better person.

In many ways, that single metaphor summarises the four fruits of meditation. His metaphor captures beautifully the journey from the head to the heart, from an ego-centric way of seeing to a God-centred way, from a focus on the egoic self to seeing the world from the perspective of the true-self. It captures how meditation nourishes the spirit and inspires one towards contemplative action, towards living life with ever-greater authenticity: impelling the individual to search for truth and to live by what he or she finds. It captures the essence of what very many of the children were pointing to: that meditation gives rise to a deep inner experience, a search for ultimate meaning and value, for an authentic compass to guide how they engage in all of their relationships – with themselves, one another, all of creation and the source of all.

Meditation Builds Community Self-Presence

The four fruits discussed above apply to the children individually. But my research also suggests that, where meditation is practised on a whole-school basis, it bears fruit for the whole school community also in terms of experiencing a deep sense of community self-presence. On a very practical level, Jessica (9) observed:

> We are all the same in meditation. It doesn't make me think 'Well, that person is better than me' and it doesn't make me feel like I'm better than anybody else. It makes me feel that I fit in with everybody else.

Whole-school silence also gives expression to the mysterious unity of the practice at a deeper level. Freeman suggests that there are many layers of silence in meditation: silence of the tongue, the whole body, the mind and the spirit.[3] The first kind of silence arises as the practitioner chooses not to speak or do anything to disrupt the silence. Such a silence creates a valuable space, especially when one is in danger of becoming caught up in one's emotions.[4] The conversations with the children show that meditation makes them mindful not alone of their own hurts and worries, but also their own transgressions, times when they have caused offence or hurt another's feelings. Practising silence alerts one to the possibility that silence may be the most suitable response in some situations. The second layer of silence is that of the whole body, as the practitioner commits to be still for the length of the meditation. Meditation, often quite quickly, leads to body-consciousness as the mind becomes more still. For example, children experienced a desire to scratch an itch but they also learned that such a desire can be resisted and that not every itch needs to be scratched. As Norah (10) observed: 'I learned that if I don't scratch it, it just goes away'. An 'itch' may be metaphorical as well as physical and children realise that most desires are temporary and will disappear if ignored; on the other hand, they come to realise too that desire can be stoked by feeding it with attention. The fact that they practised meditation in class groups on a whole-school basis also helped them to resist such 'itching' because they were aware they would be disturbing others if they gave in and broke the silence. In this way, the children come to know, perceptually if not yet conceptually, that the self-restraint involved in physical stillness can be a first step in transcending desire. It also makes a contribution to building a sense of community self-presence.

The wisdom traditions advise that stillness of body promotes stillness of mind, which is the third layer of silence referred to by Freeman. At the same time, feelings find expression through the body, they become embodied. Many children in this study spoke of how in meditation they 'feel more' what they are feeling. Some of the children also alluded to the importance of their whole class, even the whole-school, being involved in meditation at the same time. There was a sense of meditation as a whole-school embodiment. The fact that a whole school community chooses to sit together in silence creates a communal mindset that promotes a sense of stillness, as it were, in the body of the whole school community. Stillness and silence hold special significance as a group meditates. The more silent each person is, the more everyone is helped to maintain it and the more the silence becomes a communal silence. Communal silence can make a huge contribution to the building of community. Communal silence adds an inexpressible depth to the silence of the mind and is conducive to silence of the spirit, which is the fourth level of silence. It arises from 'being able to remain still and silent, moved only by silence itself, not by any thought, even the most subtle thought about silence'.[5] Ultimately, this silence of the spirit has a positive agency. Philo Hove describes this agency as follows:

> It transcends the mere absence of speech to achieve a presence of rich inner stillness. Instead of being yet another element of practice to make effort towards, there is now an effortlessness to it. In this case, the silence achieves an agency of its own; that is, rather than something I am doing, it becomes something I am.[6]

In the context of a whole school community, it becomes something the whole community does, giving expression to what the school is as a community at the very deepest level. Meditation is, in essence, about effortless intention to simply be what one truly is. Until it is experienced, it is difficult to comprehend how effortless intention can have such rich agency; indeed, it is ultimately something that one apprehends rather than comprehends. To an outside observer, meditation may initially present as a very self-centred activity; however, from a spiritual perspective, it is not a retreat from the world, but a movement towards something, towards Ultimate Reality. While it may appear to an observer as a static state, it is in fact very dynamic, but the dynamism lies beneath the surface of things, beneath the stillness, at a level of consciousness deeper than self-consciousness.

When a whole class or a whole school engages in silence together, it generates a commitment to a shared value and contributes to a strong sense of belonging to the school as a community rather than an institution and to understanding the inter-being of all of creation. Popular discourse in postmodern secular society tends to favour the rights of the individual over that of the community. It tends to emphasise the importance of fashioning an authentic life for oneself while a faith-based practice like meditation values just as much the common good of all. Meditation promotes the recognition that the true-self in every individual has a common source in God. As a spiritual practice, meditation acknowledges the equality of all human beings and values service toward the common good over personal gain.

Adrian (11) gave a very rich description of how he felt because the whole school meditated together:

It feels like everyone is one. We're all together and still it feels like there is just no one. It feels like no one is around you, as if everyone is where you are now. And God is in the presence.

So, it is more than merely building a sense of community but it builds an awareness of the school as a faith community, which acknowledges divine presence and its relationship as a community to that presence. The communal silence arises and deepens as the attention of every child is focused on silently repeating and 'listening to' their sacred word.

Adrian's words point very simply and very beautifully to the movement of the psyche from the egoic and dualistic 'I am' to the great non-dual 'I AM', which encompasses all. Through the whole-school practice, each child becomes aware – however dimly – of his or her mysterious connection with everyone else and with the divine. I found again and again throughout the research that it is a remarkable experience to be present in a school that is voluntarily silent. Adrian's comments, that it feels like 'everyone is where you are now' and 'everyone is one … and God is in the presence', capture some of the richness, depth and mystery of the group experience.

Graphic Representation of the Experience, Benefits and Fruits of Meditation

As this presentation of the insights gained from my research

133

draws to a close, the key insights gained through my research are represented graphically and metaphorically in Figure 4.4 on the next page. The motifs of the experience of meditation, of a specific session of meditation, which we explored in chapter three are portrayed as the roots of a tree, representing the life of the person. The regular experience of these motifs through the practice of meditation harnesses an energy that gives rise to the longer-term benefits and fruits of meditation, which are depicted as bursting forth from its crown. It is deliberately shaped to resemble the form of the two hemispheres of the human brain. The psychological benefits of meditation, which we explored in chapter one, are shown as leaves, on the left-hand side of the crown, corresponding to the pragmatic left hemisphere of the brain, the centre of conceptual knowledge. And the deeper spiritual fruits, which we explored in chapter four are shown as fruit on the right-hand side of the tree, corresponding to the more creative right hemisphere of the brain, the centre of perceptual knowledge. This image picks up on Kate's insight, quoted above, in which she saw the blossoms budding on a tree as representing the flourishing of the human spirit.

Figure 4.4 How Children Experience Meditation, its Benefits and Spiritual Fruits

Practice Five

Now that you have a better understanding of what it means to meditate, why not set the timer on your phone for twelve minutes and enjoy a twelve-minute meditation.

Follow the instructions in practice two (page 62) but this time extend your period of meditation to twelve minutes.

135

Endnotes

1. Christie, *Coming Home: A Guide to Teaching Christian Meditation to Children*, 33. These are in addition to the practical benefits of reducing stress, increasing their sense of well-being and harmony and building community.

2. Van Manen observes, 'Perception through sight, hearing, and touch is first of all primal. Similarly, there is the body knowledge that guides us through what we do. And we do not always "know" what we know. It is the unknowing consciousness, a non-cognitive knowing, that guides much of our daily doing and acting.' Max van Manen, *Phenomonology of Practice: Meaning-Giving Methods in Phenomenological Research and Writing*, Walnut Creek, CA: Left Coast Press, Inc., 2014, Kindle Locations 1240–2.

3. Laurence Freeman, Lenten Reflection, 1 March 2016, us4.campaign-archive2.com/?u=c3f683a744ee71a2a6032f4bc&id=27491f01f1&e=b69624270f

4. Thoughtlessness seems to find particular expression, often hurtful and damaging, in social media today.

5. Laurence Freeman, Lenten Reflection, 1 March 2016, us4.campaign-archive2.com/?u=c3f683a744ee71a2a6032f4bc&id=27491f01f1&e=b69624270f

6. Philo Hove, 'Learning Retreat Meditation' in Max van Manen (ed.), *Writing in the Dark: Phenomenological Studies in Interpretive Inquiry*, Walnut Creek, CA: Left Coast Press, 2015, p. 211.

Chapter Five

Introducing Children to Meditation

This chapter contains three simple lessons for introducing meditation to children. It was written initially for introducing the practice to children in the classroom but the lessons can be used equally well in any other communal or home setting. They are brief and to the point because the practice is in essence experiential. While it is helpful to have a way of introducing it to children, and indeed to adults who are attempting it for the first time, there is no need for a complicated set of instructions. Each lesson allows for some dialogue and the content of such dialogue will, of course, depend on the age, maturity and life experience of the children involved.

The lessons are presented in a deliberate sequence. Lesson one introduces the children to meditation as a universal practice in all its simplicity – the focus is on doing it. Lesson two introduces the children to the benefits of meditation as children describe them and lesson three explores the deeper, spiritual fruits of the practice as described by children and refers also to meditation in the Christian tradition. It can be adapted by the teacher or parent to refer to any tradition. The intention is to allow a period of several weeks – even a month – between the lessons, so that the children have an opportunity to really tune in to their personal experience of the practice, and its benefits and fruits.

Lesson one is presented in a way that allows you, if you wish, to follow it verbatim. It will, of course, need to be adapted somewhat to suit the ages of the children in your care, but it has been delivered very successfully to children aged five to twelve years old. Lessons two and three are not presented in that verbatim style but as a series of discussion points which you can use as the basis for the lesson.

Note: In chapter one we explored whether there are circumstances in which meditation might have a negative effect. It is possible, however unlikely, that a child might get upset over a bereavement or something that is going on in their life that comes to the surface in the silence of meditation. It is important that the teacher would have considered beforehand how to handle it with tact and discretion, so they are not taken by surprise.

Lesson One | How to Meditate

Aim: To introduce children to the simplicity of meditation. This first lesson is designed as an opening presentation to get the children started on the meditation path. It treats of meditation as a general, widespread, secular practice – there is no mention of God.

Learning Outcomes: Children will know how to be still and silent in meditation and will have experienced it in practice. They will appreciate that thoughts will inevitably arise and will know how to return to repeating their word as an aid to letting go of their thoughts.

Key Elements

- Meditation is about being still – in body and in mind
- What does it mean to be still in body?
- What does it mean to be still in mind?
- To still our thoughts, we focus on something else. We will use a word, Maranatha (or an alternative)
- Glitter Jar as a metaphor for a busy mind (optional)
- Meditation Instructions
- We meditate because meditation is good for us (refer to 'settled' glitter jar)

1. Today we are going to learn something new. We are going to learn how to meditate. I wonder has anyone done it before?

[*If so, engage gently with the child or children about their experience without going into very much detail.*]

We will start our meditation shortly. We will do it first and then we'll talk about why it's good for you. It is very different to what you normally do in class because what we are going to do is to be very still and quiet. We are going to do nothing but meditate.

I invite you all to try to be very still in body and mind. Meditation is really good for you because it gives you a break from working all the time. It gives us a break from that busy feeling. It's really nice to take a break. So, shall we do that in a moment?

When we meditate we try to be still in our body and still in our mind. But what does that mean?

2. What does it mean if you are still in your body?

[*Wait for the children to raise their hands and respond – treat each contribution with genuine appreciation. Then ask for examples of what it means if we are not still in our body and again treat each contribution with great respect. Then demonstrate. Begin, for example, by sitting straight and still but lightly tapping your foot on the floor and ask if that is being still in body! Then sit still, but wiggle your fingers all the time or fiddle with your watch or a piece of jewellery and ask if that is being still in body. This discussion will clarify for the children, in a friendly way, what it means to be still in body.*]

Is it easy to be still in your body? Let's try it for thirty seconds. We will try to be very still and not move a muscle. Let's close our eyes, if you are comfortable with that, and see if we can hear anything moving. Let's try it for thirty seconds until I invite you to open your eyes again.

[*Afterwards, compliment the children on how they meditated and on the silence that helped everyone to meditate. Ask them if it was easy or hard to do. After a brief chat, conclude by noting that most people find it fairly easy to be still in body. But assure them that if they found it hard, not to worry – it will get easier.*]

3. Okay. Let's try something now that's a bit harder. Let's see if we can be still in our minds! What does that mean to be still in our minds? Let's close our eyes, if you are okay with that, and see what happens if we try to be still in our mind. Let's try it for thirty seconds until I invite you to open your eyes again.

How was that? Was it hard or easy? I see that some found it easy, but most people find it hard to still their mind.

[*Talk with them a little about their experience, noting that adults too generally find it very difficult to still the mind.*]

It's hard, isn't it? It's very hard to stop thinking! Ideas just keep popping into your head. Have you ever brought a dog for a walk? Did you notice that they keep stopping to sniff every plant and flower? Our minds are a bit like that, always looking for something new to think about. Some people call it 'Monkey Mind' – because thoughts are like a monkey jumping from branch to branch. Can anyone suggest how we might try to stop our mind from wandering so much? What could we do to help keep our minds more still?

[*Some children may volunteer an answer. If they do, treat each response with great respect and tease out its potential for stilling the mind.*]

There are different things we could do, but one of the best is to focus our minds on something else.

4. Here's a trick to stop your mind from jumping about. We will give it something else to do. We won't think about anything, we'll just repeat a single word over and over again. Whenever we find we are thinking, we'll go back to the word. We'll use a word you've never used before: Maranatha.

[*This word comes from the Christian tradition but you can choose a word from any tradition. If teaching in a faith-based school, please choose a word from that faith tradition or if teaching meditation to children in a wholly secular context choose a neutral word or phrase such as 'peace to all'.*]

Maranatha is a big word but we will say it as if it is four small words: Ma-ra-na-tha

[*Write the word on a whiteboard or a flipchart so they can see it.*]

Will you say that with me, nice and slowly? Ma-ra-na-tha. When we meditate we will say it silently without speaking or moving our lips – just in our heads. You can say it at whatever pace suits you, just not too fast. One young boy told me recently he likes to say it at the speed of the ticking of a clock: Ma…Ra…Na… Tha.

It's a strange word, isn't it? And that is good. You don't know what it means yet (although I'll tell you later) and that means it doesn't make you think about anything. So that helps. Imagine if I asked you to use the word 'sausages'. Why might that not be a good idea?

[*Engage with the children exploring how a word like 'sausages' makes us think of food and may even have us hearing the sizzle of sausages frying in the pan. It brings thoughts to our minds and that's exactly what we don't want to do when we meditate.*]

In a moment, I will put on a CD and we can all listen carefully and follow the instructions.

143

[The Meditation with Children Project in Ireland has prepared a CD for introducing meditation to children. The tracks from the CD are available from their website.]

Alternatively, say that you will give them simple instructions in a moment.

5. *[If you have easy access to a glitter jar or can make one yourself, then it may be helpful to introduce one at this stage but it is by no means necessary.]*

Before we meditate, can I ask if you have seen a glitter jar before? It contains lots of loose glitter in a liquid. What will happen when I shake the jar?

[As always, treat their responses with respect.]

Let's try it. What do you think will happen in the glitter jar while we meditate? Okay, let's put the jar down and we will come back to it after meditation.

[Place the jar out of sight so it won't be a distraction for the children during meditation.]

Note: In naming the meditation project in the schools we called it the Meditation *with* Children project and that, of course, is the ideal. Parents introducing the practice to children should, of course, meditate with them. The teacher must be seen to honour the

meditation practice but is still responsible for all of
the children in their care and cannot, therefore, close
their eyes and meditate with their eyes closed. The
teacher has a responsibility to ensure the safety of all
of the children during every meditation period, so
they must remain fully alert to their responsibilities.
However, it is important that the teacher honours
the practice by remaining quiet and still, just like
the children. Any unnecessary movement will be
distracting and will make it difficult for the children
to truly settle in to the practice.

Hints

In many schools nowadays, children sit four to six
around a table, facing one another.

- Many teachers find it helpful to ask the children to pull
  their chair back a little from the table – so they won't
  fidget with anything on it. In fact, some teachers take
  care to leave each table bare for meditation.
- Many also ask the children to turn their chairs around
  so everybody is facing the top of the class. This has
  the advantage that if any child opens their eyes during
  meditation, they won't find another child staring back
  at them!
- When people meditate from a faith-based perspective,
  they often light a candle (battery operated, for safety) on
  the teacher's table or a special small table, to represent
  the presence of the divine and to remind themselves

about their intention to be still and silent in God's presence. That can be introduced at a later stage if you wish to do so, after lesson three. But you might also do it now, without alluding to its religious symbolism. For example, we often light candles for special occasions, such as if we are having a family meal or celebrating a birthday. When you go into a restaurant you will often find that each table has a candle and some flowers to mark the fact that those eating together are taking time out to relax and share some time together. For the same reason, you could have a small bunch of flowers on the table also, if you wish. But neither is strictly necessary.

6. [*Before beginning the meditation, say a word to the children about your role during it.*]

While we are meditating I remain responsible for every child in this class and for making sure that each one of you can meditate quietly, safely and happily. So while I will say the word in my mind, I will have to keep my eyes open. But I will sit here quietly and, like you, I won't do anything to disturb the quiet. If someone is fidgeting or moving or making a small noise and doesn't know it, I will just tap you gently on the shoulder to remind you to be still and quiet. Is that okay? Right, let's begin.

[*Alternatively, you may choose to do the introduction yourself. The following is the wording from the CD.*]

Now, children, we are going to meditate together.
We begin by closing our eyes and placing our feet
firmly on the floor.
Check that you are sitting up straight in your chair
with your hands on your lap or your knees.
Become aware of the sounds in the room, then let
them go.
Become aware of the sounds outside, then let them go.
Become aware of any thoughts arising in your mind,
then let them go.
Happy thoughts or sad thoughts, kind thoughts or
angry thoughts,
Calm thoughts or worried thoughts, just for now, let
them go.
Imagine placing them on a leaf in a stream and now
allow the leaf to float down the stream, carrying your
thoughts with them. Let them drift away.

[In a Christian school you might add the following:

Christians believe that when you meditate you open your
heart to God, who fills you with his love. You will now
hear a few lines of the song 'Into the Quiet'.]

When the meditation bell rings three times, begin to
recite your word. Say Ma-ra-na-tha as if it were four
short words. Say it silently in your mind so no one else
will hear a thing.
Say it slowly and lovingly: Ma-ra-na-tha.

When thoughts pop into your head, become aware of
them, acknowledge them but don't entertain them.
Just smile and let them drift away, and return gently to
your word: Ma-ra-na-tha.
Keep doing this until the meditation bell rings again
at the end of the meditation. Notice how the gong
reverberates. Listen to the final gong until you can
hear it no longer and then open your eyes again.

7. [*After meditation explain briefly to the children why people
    meditate.*]

Meditation is really good for you. There are lots of
reasons why meditation is good for you.

[*If you introduced the glitter jar, you can refer to it here.*]

The glitter jar may give us one idea why. Do you
remember that we shook the glitter jar before we
started meditating? Let's look and see what has
happened? When we shook the jar, it became all
swirly, with the stars flying about in all directions. Our
minds can get like that too when we have too much
going on. The glitter swirling around the jar is a little
bit like our thoughts racing in our heads. Imagine
each piece of glitter is a thought. When we are under
pressure they all get jumbled up together so we can't
even think straight. But while we were meditating the
jar calmed down. All the glitter settled and the liquid

became clear and calm. The glitter stopped swirling around and the jar became clear again. When the jar sits still, everything calms down. It's the same with us.

[If you did not introduce the glitter jar, continue as follows.]

When we sit, still in body and mind, everything calms down – our body and our thoughts – and, after meditation, we are able to think more clearly. We will talk more about why meditation is good for us the next day. In the meantime, we will practise our meditation every day or every few days. And when we are more used to it we will come back and talk about how it helps us.

Regular Practice

Over the next few weeks meditate often with your child or class group – at least twice a week but every day if possible. All you need to do is explain that you are now going to meditate together. Then read the meditation instructions or, if you have downloaded it, play the appropriate track from the CD or give a brief introduction yourself. Many schools start with two minutes and work up to the average for the class (children can meditate for one minute per year of age). Once the children have become used to the introduction you can shorten it, limiting it to the bare instructions.

It is highly desirable in a school that the whole school meditates at the same time. As the older children get used to it, they can extend the time and meditate for a little longer than the others, but it is ideal that all classes begin together. There is something deeply inspiring about the silence and stillness that falls over a school as everybody meditates. Although it may seem passive to an outsider, it is a very dynamic activity.

Lesson Two | Why People Meditate: The Benefits of Meditation

It is important that children will have experienced meditation on a regular basis in the period between lessons one and two. It is advisable that children meditate at least twice each week as a class group, ideally, as a whole school, and preferably more often. Children should also be advised to meditate at home and to invite their parents to meditate with them. By now children will have developed their own practical understanding of what it is like to meditate and they will have experienced some of its benefits for themselves, although they may not yet have reflected on them.

Aim: To introduce children to the benefits of meditation. This lesson continues to refer to meditation as a universal practice – there is no mention of God.

Learning Outcomes: Children will have learned about the benefits of meditation as described by children and will have had an opportunity to discuss their own experience of its benefits. They will be able to say why it can be good for people to meditate.

It is best to do this lesson after a meditation session, so on that day set aside a little extra time for reflection and discussion with the children immediately after the meditation session.

Key Elements

- Did you feel better after meditation? (Glitter Jar)
- Why do people meditate? How does meditation help people?
- What other children say about the benefits of meditation:
  - You Let Go of All the Drama
  - You Feel Calm and Relaxed
  - You Have More Energy and Confidence
  - You Make Better Decisions

Lesson one was written in a style that allows a parent or teacher to follow it verbatim if they wish. Lessons two and three are presented differently, as a series of key points to be made. These can form the basis of a lesson plan or they could be spread over a number of lessons. The tone and language should be adapted to suit the ages and needs of the children.

1. You might begin the discussion by saying that the children have been meditating now for a while and asking what they think of it. Ask if they feel better after meditation. If you had introduced the glitter jar in the first lesson or subsequently, you might remind them about it (or introduce it now) and recall how it symbolises the way that meditation calms our bodies and gives us a break from our thoughts.

    You might then ask if there are other ways in which meditation might help us. 'Wondering' questions are really good for getting children to open up about their experience, so ask, 'I wonder how you feel meditation helps?' However, never direct the question at a particular child. Some children may be very willing to talk about it but others may not. My research found that, as a general rule, children don't talk to one another readily about such things.

2. It may be more helpful to phrase the question indirectly, e.g. 'I wonder why people meditate? Why do you think people meditate?' Listen respectfully to what they say, honouring their privacy and sensitivities. The intention here is not that the children engage in a wide-ranging discussion, but that they are given an opportunity to say something about their experience if they wish and an opportunity is created to share with them some information about the benefits of meditation. You can summarise what they are saying on the whiteboard if you wish, but it's not necessary to do so.

3. After a while, bring that part of the discussion to a close, explaining that others have spoken with children about what they think of meditation and how they benefit from it and that you are going to look at what they said. Depending on the length of the previous discussion with the class and the time available now, you can choose to continue with the next part of this lesson or defer it to the next meditation day.

The things that other children say about the benefits of meditation are shown in Figure 5.1, which you can display.[1]

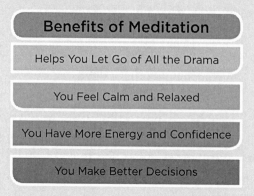

Figure 5.1 The Benefits of Meditation According to Children

There are lots of benefits to meditation and there is no one right way to describe them. The diagram presents how the children in my study described the benefits of meditation as they experienced them. If I spoke to a different group of children, they might have expressed them differently. My research was conducted in a particular context in primary schools in the cultural context of Ireland.

You may spend a little while comparing what the children told you from their own experience to what appears on the diagram and you can make connections between them. Over the next few paragraphs I will tease out what the children said, as much as possible in child-friendly language. You may present this as simply as you think fit for the group of children in your care. Benefits were identified under the four headings shown in Figure 5.1 above. These benefits were teased out in detail in chapter one and are summarised as bullet points below.

Helps You Let Go of All the Drama

- Meditation helps children to let go of all the drama of a busy school day.
- When we take time out to meditate, we can let go of everything that is bothering us, even for a few minutes and that can be enough to clear the mind and let go of anxiety and worry.
- Meditation is all about letting go. Every time we meditate we build up our 'letting go' muscle – of course, it's not a muscle, it's more of an attitude. As we practise letting go of our thoughts, we also learn to let go of our worries, our fears, and all the things that make us stressed.
- Many children commented that they meditated before or during sports competitions, even before tests in school.

You Feel Calm and Relaxed

- Meditation makes children feel really calm and relaxed. Sometimes when we are under pressure, even the smallest thing can upset us. But when we meditate we no longer feel overwhelmed by what happens to us, no longer as angry when something goes wrong.
- That means too that we are able to think more clearly and are more likely to get things right, to make fewer mistakes.
- Sometimes when we are tense and uptight, we put up barriers, we don't let others in. But when we are calm and relaxed, we are more open to people, more open to seeing things differently, more open even to trying new things.

- Lots of children said they loved the peace and quiet of the classroom during meditation. Normally, the classroom is a busy, noisy, boisterous space and it changes the whole atmosphere when everybody calms down at the same time.

You Have More Energy and Confidence

- Children are sometimes surprised to find that after meditation they have more energy and confidence. When we meditate, it's as if we wipe the slate clean and then we have space for something new and that gives us the energy to start again.
- Children also found that it made them more confident, more able to take on something new. They are more confident about putting their hand up to answer questions. They are less worried about getting it wrong and realise it isn't about getting the right answer every time, but being willing to look for the right answer.
- Many children find that they get more work done in a lesson after meditation. It helps them to pay attention, to concentrate.
- Some teachers allow the children to meditate before they do their spelling test because as well as making them calm and relaxed about the test, it also gives them more confidence.

You Make Better Decisions

- Children also say that meditation helps them to make better decisions. They don't rush into things as quickly as they used to. Meditation makes them more aware of their feelings and they are able to decide to hold back and let things calm down where before they might have rushed in and made things worse.

- Even when the children did overreact to something, meditation seemed to have given them the ability to see their mistake more readily and they learned to apologise and start again.

It may be helpful at the end of this lesson to go back to the diagram and recall the four benefits of meditation as children describe them. It might be interesting to invite the children to share their understanding of the benefits of meditation through a drawing, a poster or a poem as part of classwork or voluntary homework.

Lesson Three | Why People Meditate: The Fruits of Meditation

Aim: To introduce children to meditation as a spiritual practice and to explore the spiritual fruits of meditation. This lesson introduces meditation as a spiritual practice, with a particular focus on the Christian tradition. However, it can be adapted by teachers and parents to refer to any tradition.

Learning Outcomes: Children will understand that many people meditate as part of their religion (or their spiritual practice), in order to simply be with God. They will be familiar with the inner fruits of meditation as described by children and will have had an opportunity to discuss their own experience of its fruits. In Christian terms, they will be able to relate its fruits to the fruits of the Spirit as described by St Paul.

Key Elements
- Some people meditate to spend time with God.
- As well as having practical benefits, meditation also has deep inner fruits.
- What other children say about the fruits of meditation:
  - You Can Be Yourself
  - You Feel the Goodness Deep Inside
  - You Come Closer to God
  - You Become a Kinder Person

Note: Chapter one outlined the Christian tradition of meditation. In chapter two we explored the fruits of meditation as described in the Christian tradition and in chapter four we detailed how children described the spiritual fruits. It may be helpful to review that material before teaching this lesson.

1. Meditation is an important part of many religions in different parts of the world. It is also an important part the Christian religion. Prayer is important to Christians and meditation is a form of silent prayer. Usually when we pray we use words. We thank God for things, we pray that people will not suffer from war or hunger, we pray for people who are not as fortunate as ourselves, we ask God to help them and we promise to do what we can to help.

   But we don't have to use words when we pray. We can simply choose to be with God, with Jesus. That's what we do in meditation – we open our hearts to God and he fills us with his love. Meditation is often called the prayer to the heart. And after meditation we show love to all around us. When we meditate, we sit with Jesus, in his company, without saying anything with our voice or in our minds. Instead, we let our heart do the 'talking'. God created each of us and he knows us better than we know ourselves. There is a verse in the Bible that says, 'Be still and know that I am God.' When we meditate in silence we can feel that in our hearts.

2. Children meditate so they can spend time with God, with Jesus, in a special way. Children who do this regularly find that meditation changes them. The change happens very quietly and slowly – not during meditation but after you have been meditating regularly for a while. Meditation strengthens our sense of God in everything – in ourselves, in one another, in our families, in nature, in other creatures. Meditation makes us realise we are all in this together, that we are all children of God.

3. Christians believe that meditation leads to deep inner fruits, to human flourishing. Figure 5.2 depicts how children describe the fruits of meditation. Because these fruits are teased out in detail in chapter four, they are merely summarised as bullet points here.

Figure 5.2 The Fruits of Meditation According to Children

You Can Be Yourself

- Lots of children say that meditation helps them to be themselves, to be true to themselves. You might ask the children what they think is meant by that.

- Many children say that meditation brings them deeper inside themselves. You might ask, 'Does that make sense to you? How would you say that, in your own words, from your experience of meditation?'
- Children also say that meditation makes them realise that everybody is different and that each person is already perfect just as they are. Meditation helps them to realise that they can be themselves.
- Other children say that meditation helps them to get in touch with their own feelings more, to 'feel their feelings' more. So, instead of getting caught up in their anger, they are aware that they are getting caught up in it. They can see that their anger, and not their best self, is in the driving seat, directing their behaviour. And they can change that.
- When somebody else is very angry with them, the children are able to stand back and figure out that that person's behaviour is driven by their anger and that their behaviour doesn't represent who they really are.

You Feel the Goodness Deep Inside

- Lots of the children say that meditation makes them feel the goodness deep inside themselves. As they let go of their thoughts, meditation moves them away from their heads and into their hearts. You might ask, 'Do you know what I mean by that? How would you describe that in your own words?'
- Speaking about meditation, one child said, 'Meditation makes me realise that when someone is behaving badly, there is still goodness inside them but because they are

161

upset they just can't see it. If they meditated they might see it.'

- Another child said that when he is not meditating he tends to follow his head but when he meditates he follows his heart. You might ask, 'What do you think he meant by that? Can you think of any time when you felt like that?'

- One young girl said that when she discovered the goodness inside of herself it was like discovering a secret garden. It was there all the time but she hadn't really appreciated it until she started to meditate.

- The Christian faith tells us that the Holy Spirit dwells in every person. And the Gospels show us that Jesus always saw the goodness in everyone. Throughout his life, he came to know his true-self. And he shows us how to be true to ourselves by following his example, how to follow our heart, how to let our goodness show. Meditation grows this way of seeing and being in our hearts.

You Come Closer to God

- When we sit in meditation, in silence, still in body and still in mind, we are not doing anything. We are just being ourselves, being with God. Meditation is a time to simply sit with God, with Jesus.

- For Christians, meditation is a silent way of praying. When we meditate we don't think about anything and we don't say anything, apart from our sacred word. In meditation, we can be with Jesus, not to talk to him but simply to be with him.

- Saint John of the Cross said, 'Silence is God's first language.' You might ask, 'I wonder what that means? How can you communicate with someone who can't hear? Or relate to someone who can't speak? Usually we communicate with people using words. But can you think of ways we can relate to someone who is deaf? By smiling, perhaps, to show them we are happy to see them? By touch, maybe giving them a hug? How do we communicate with a baby who is too small to understand words? With hugs and kisses or holding them lovingly and protectively. Have you ever been with a pet dog or cat and felt really close to them even without saying a word or touching them? Just being with them.'

- It's the same with God. We can speak to him without using words. We can feel really close to him, really loved by him and love him back, in our hearts. We can feel Jesus' love for us without having to hear him say it out loud. And we know he can understand the love we have for him and for our friends without us having to say it.

- One child said, 'There is a part of God in everyone's heart.' You might ask, 'I wonder what she meant by that?' Our faith tells us that God created each one of us in his image; so, deep inside, that is who we really are. And when we meditate we can feel that very deeply. When we meditate, we acknowledge that God is always present to us, though sometimes we are too busy to notice his presence, and we come to enjoy the chance to make ourselves present for the time of meditation.

- Children understand the use of symbols and that at times of prayer people often use a candle to symbolise the presence of God. Norah (10) lights a candle when she meditates at home and she imagines when they meditate in school that it's as if each person is a lighted candle and '[God] flies into each candle, leaving hope in each one'. The symbolism may help to mark the silence as a sacred silence rather than the mere absence of sound.[2]

John Main also makes use of the imagery of a candle flame, asking us to imagine that as we race through our busy lives, there is a candle in our hearts and because we are moving at such high speed, this candle is always in danger of going out. But when we sit down in the stillness and silence of meditation, in the real presence, then the flame begins to burn brightly.[3]

- Through such symbols and stories, we may begin to understand ourselves and others in terms of light, energy, warmth and love, all of which are made manifest in meditation.
- Some children say that when they meditate they feel very close to people they knew who loved them but who have died. Some even say that in meditation they feel very close to pets who have passed away. Meditation helps us to connect with God and with those we love, whether they are still with us or have passed on from this world.
- Lots of children say that they love it when the whole school meditates together. It makes them feel that

everybody is equal. They realise that meditation is something that every child and adult can do equally well. Nobody is better or worse at meditation than anyone else. Everybody is doing the same thing, saying their word and letting go of their thoughts, over and over again. Everybody is just being with God. One child said, 'When we meditate it feels like everyone is one ... as if everyone is where you are now. And God is in the Presence.' You might ask, 'I wonder what he meant by that? What do you think? How do you experience being close to God in meditation?'

You Become a Kinder Person

- Because you have discovered the goodness inside yourself and the same goodness in others, you are able to be kinder to yourself, to your friends, and to others in your class and school that you don't normally play with.
- Because you have come to realise who you really are and can be yourself, you are able to let others be themselves too. You don't put pressure on others to be the way you want them to be. You accept them for who they are.
- You realise everybody doesn't have to be the same and that everybody is equal, but different. And that allows you to be kinder to them and to yourself. Sometimes we can be very hard on ourselves and others but meditation makes us realise that everybody makes mistakes – that's how people learn. And realising that makes us kinder to ourselves and to others.
- Jesus said a lot of things that showed how kind and loving

he was. He was asked once what was most important and he reminded us that we should love God and love our neighbour. That's the most important thing in life – to be loving, to love one another, including ourselves.

• When we see the goodness in ourselves and in others, when we realise that is who we really are, then loving ourselves and loving others isn't a big thing at all. Meditation helps us to care for one another, to look out for one another – especially anyone who is being left out or who is having a hard time. It's easy because that is who we really are, deep inside. We just have to let it show.

To conclude the lesson, you might like to sum up the four things that children say about the fruits of meditation. It lets our goodness show and shine. It helps you to be yourself, to feel the goodness inside, to come closer to God, to Jesus. And all of that makes you a kinder person because it guides you to love God and one another. We show that we love the other person as Jesus does by our actions.[4]

These four fruits of meditation might be described as 'Be-Attitudes'. Before responding to any situation think:

Before You Act:
Be Yourself
Be Aware of the Goodness Within
Be with God
Be a Kinder Person

I suggest that in the weeks following this lesson, you seek opportunities to reinforce these fruits. When something happens in the school or the class that touches on any of the fruits, you might use the opportunity to link the issue to meditation and its fruits. The story of the Good Samaritan is a good example of the Be-Attitudes. You might set aside some time a few weeks after this lesson, someday before or after meditation, to reflect briefly on the parable of the Good Samaritan. Or you could just mention it and return to it another day. For example, you might ask the children if they are familiar with the story and get them to describe it, or read it to them. And then ask them what has the story got to do with meditation? The link, of course, lies in the fact that the Good Samaritan saw clearly what needed to be done. And he believed in the Be-Attitudes. He saw the injured man and he felt very sorry for him. Because he saw the goodness in himself, he saw the goodness in the man who was beaten by the robbers also. Because he recognised the goodness in him, because he recognised that they were intimately connected through God, he acted out of the Be-Attitudes and he gave freely of himself. He responded to the man in need and he did something positive to help. Just like Jesus did every time he healed the sick, the blind and the lame. But the priest and the Levi, who were supposed to be holy men, didn't see clearly. They failed to see God in the injured man and they didn't respond appropriately to the situation.

Earlier we saw that Aideen (11) realised that some people work at enhancing their inner God and others don't. Meditation helps us to enhance our inner God, to discover our true-self, who we really are. And when we do, we begin to live out of that way of seeing. We begin to see everything clearly and we respond as the situation calls for. Saint Paul describes this as 'putting on the mind of Christ' (Phil 2:5; 1 Cor 2:16). That's another way of describing the Be-Attitudes.

In the follow-up lesson, or during RE class, it may be appropriate to link meditation and the fruits of the Spirit, which are described by St Paul in Galatians (5:22) as love, joy, peace, forbearance, kindness, goodness, faithfulness, gentleness and self-control.

Note: From this lesson onwards, you might like to light a candle (battery operated, for safety) and place it on a small table or sacred space in the room. You may add flowers if you wish. You can allude to the candle saying that it is a symbol of God's presence in the room during meditation, a symbol of the divine spark within every one of us, of our intention to be still and silent in God's presence during meditation – not talking to him or thinking about him, but simply being with him, lovingly. And remind the children that as we sit in stillness and silence in meditation, God fills our hearts with his love. Meditation fills us with the sacred energy of love.

Note: In the context of a Christian school or family, it is important to remind children from time to time that meditation is seen in the Christian tradition as a very deep form of silent prayer where we simply chose to spend time with God. We simply sit with him in stillness and silence. At other times, we may pray to God with words. We may thank him for all that is going well in our lives and families, we may pray for those who need God's help – family members or friends who are ill or in pain, those suffering from the loss of loved ones – or we might ask God to help those who are most in need – those who are homeless or for refugees who are fleeing war, poverty and famine. Praying like that is, of course, very important. But meditation is a different kind of prayer. It is a form of silent, imageless, wordless prayer where we simply sit with Jesus. We get to know about Jesus through our religious education class but we get close to him through prayer and meditation.

From this lesson onwards, you can speak of meditation as a universal practice that has become very popular in society (often referred to as 'mindfulness') but which, for many, is also a deeply spiritual practice that helps us to be ourselves and brings us closer to God. Explain that in the Christian tradition, the intention is to be still and silent in God's presence. If you have children of no faith in your group, they can continue to meditate as a secular, mindfulness practice and may choose a word acceptable to them that has no spiritual symbolism, for example, 'peace', 'joy', 'love', or a combination of them. Children of a different faith can use a word from their own faith tradition, in consultation with their parents.

Practice Six

Now that you have a better understanding of what it means to meditate, why not set the timer on your phone for fifteen minutes and enjoy a fifteen-minute meditation.

Follow the instructions in practice two (page 62) but this time extend your period of meditation to fifteen minutes.

Endnotes

1. This image is free to download from: www.christianmeditation.ie.

2. When facilitating an adult meditation group, I will usually have a single candle lighting throughout the welcome, introduction and meditation to symbolise that the divine is always present with us and to us. When the group begins to meditate, I light a second candle to symbolise that we are making ourselves present to God as we meditate. If I'm using real wax candles, I will use the first to light the second and I will comment on the transfer of energy as the first candle lights the second. That symbolism reminds us that we are energised in the silence as our spirit encounters the Holy Spirit – his flame makes ours burn more brightly. Indeed, as St Symeon the New Theologian expressed it, when you light 'a flame from a flame, it is the whole flame you receive'. Saint Symeon the New Theologian, 'Hymn 1' in *The Book of Mystical Chapters: Meditations on the Soul's Ascent from the Desert Fathers and Other Early Christian Contemplatives*, Boulder, CO: Shambhala Publications, 2003, p. 160.

3. Main, *The Hunger for Depth and Meaning*, Kindle Location 1670.

4. Jean Vanier once reflected on how does one bring the good news of the gospel to others, especially those who are marginalised, dispossessed and oppressed. He was very clear that it is not enough to tell them that they are loved by God, but each of us is called to show that love. See Jean Vanier, *Signs: Seven Words of Hope*, Toronto, ON: Novalis Publishing, 2014.

Chapter Six

Talking with Children about Meditation as Spiritual Experience

While the most important thing about meditation is the practice itself, it is important also to talk with children about their experience of the practice. Teachers and parents should create opportunities, every now and then, to talk with the children about how sitting in stillness and silence helps us to discover who we really are and to discover the other deep fruits of meditation. For religious education to contribute in a meaningful way to children's spiritual growth requires an opportunity for children to share their own stories.[1] A number of children in my study expressed their delight at having an opportunity to speak with me about meditation 'because there was no one else to speak to about it'. They were pleased to have the chance to talk about it 'with someone who would take it seriously'. This suggests the importance of engaging with children about their experience of meditation, its deep inner fruits, the spiritual nature of the experience and how their spirituality is nurtured through the practice. Such opportunities enable their spiritual experience to be affirmed, helping them to appropriate for themselves that which cannot be expressed

173

in words and giving them confidence in the truth of their own inner wisdom. Of course, any such conversations will need to be in language appropriate to their age and cognitive development and would need to be informed by an understanding of the nature of the spirituality of children, in particular its non-verbal expression.

While it is important to create opportunities for children to speak about their experience, they should never be put under pressure to do so. Kate Adams notes that because serious discussion of spiritual experiences is not common in daily discourse, children often feel a fear of ridicule or dismissal, and for that reason retreat into silence.[2] The children in my study confirmed that they were not in the habit of speaking to one another about meditation and some were reluctant to do so.[3] Sometimes the reason offered was very straightforward as, for example, when Frances (11) commented simply, 'It's not really one of those things that crops up in conversation.' Others, however, expressed the view that it was a deliberate choice not to talk about it. Pamela (11) explained, 'I don't say it to anyone, because I'm afraid they might think I'm weird.' Natalie (11) said, 'I think if I told anyone that I sensed God or that I was closer to God when I do meditation, I think they would laugh. So, I just keep it to myself.'

It is possible, therefore, that even if opportunities were created for discussion, children might still find it difficult to contribute because it is a deeply relational and personal matter and it is very difficult to express what one has come to realise in words. It is important to create a safe, respectful atmosphere where children who would like to share their experiences feel safe to do so, and those who choose not to share are given an absolute right to privacy.

All of the wisdom traditions express the view that the deeper, long-term fruits of the practice arise from the discipline of regular, ideally daily, meditation and this too should be explained to children. They should be encouraged to meditate outside of the context of school also so they may come to appreciate meditation as a gift that can be accessed at any time, at any age and at will.

In order to generate conversation with the children for my research, in addition to asking analogical questions such as 'If meditation was a colour what colour would it be?', there were two other methods I used that might be adapted for use at home or in the classroom. The first is photo-elicitation and the second is a method I call the Selection Box. The next two lessons explain how these methods can be used to generate conversations with children around meditation and its spiritual fruits.

Using Photo-Elicitation to Generate Conversation about Meditation

Photo-elicitation uses simple images to stimulate the children to make connections between the image and the topic under discussion. During the first interview with each child, each was given a stack of thirty laminated photographs (A4) and invited to choose the three or four that most reminded them of meditation.[4] The images, which were unrelated to the research topic, depicted a range of ordinary life situations including: adults and children, happy and sad, delighted and frustrated; nature, both calm and beautiful scenes and images of pollution; imaginative artistic drawing; images from day-to-day life, including sport, music and a traffic jam. I was careful not to use images that might be commonly regarded as symbols of spirituality or religion as this might lead the children in a particular direction. In effect, they were being asked to choose which images were the best metaphors for their experience of meditation and its benefits and fruits. The children were then asked to describe what they saw in each of their chosen images and to say why they reminded them of meditation. This enabled the children to give metaphorical expression to aspects of the experience that otherwise defy easy description.

This methodology enabled each child and the interviewer to be mutually engaged in uncovering the child's signification of meaning. The use of photo-elicitation enabled me to enter the realm of mystery with the children. I illustrated this process with some examples in chapter four when I was elucidating the fruits of meditation as experienced by the children. For example, Kate's choice of a bird sitting on a budding branch and her description of the bud as evidence that the tree's spirit was blossoming before going on to indicate that in meditation her spirit blossoms. Other children chose a colourful image of a tropical fish on a coral reef. It led some to observe how bright, colourful and happy the image was and they went on to say how meditation fills them with happiness, even joy. Others observed that the fish were free to be themselves – and that led some children to comment that meditation gives rise to a sense of inner freedom. Some went on to say directly, 'Meditation helps me to be myself.' There were many other examples of how the photo-elicitation resulted in metaphorical descriptions of the experience of meditation and its benefits and fruits.

Lesson Four | Generating Conversation about Meditation through Photo-Elicitation

Aim: To generate conversation with the children about meditation as a spiritual practice and to explore the spiritual fruits of meditation.

Learning Outcomes: Children will make metaphorical connections regarding the spiritual fruits of meditation or will hear how other children did so.

Key Elements

- Presenting children with some everyday images and asking if any of them remind them in any way of meditation.
- Facilitating a sensitive conversation with those children who wish to contribute to the discussion on meditation as a spiritual practice.

One approach to photo-elicitation in the classroom might be to show, say, six diverse images in a single slide, identifying each one by a capital letter.

1. Each child might be asked to choose one that reminds them of meditation or some aspect of it.[5]
2. The children might then be asked to write down the letter of the image they have chosen together with a brief description of the image, i.e. to say what they see in the picture. This will help to establish what aspects of it are symbolic for them.

3. The teacher might then recall that they had chosen their image because it reminded them about meditation and ask them to say why, e.g. to complete the sentence 'This picture reminds me of meditation because ...'

4. The whole exercise could be done in silence and pages collected from the children.

5. You might reflect on them overnight and report back to the children the next day summarising what you had learned but being careful not to name or embarrass any child.

6. The children might be invited to comment on your feedback if they wished to do so but they shouldn't feel under any pressure to do so. Even if no child shares their feelings or experience verbally, the fact that you have read them and commented on the exercise, stressing the fruits of meditation, may be enough to validate their experience and see that the practice is genuinely valued as having very deep potential for inner nourishment.

As noted in an earlier chapter, it is vital to listen attentively to what the children say, and this includes what they write. Be attentive for any hint of spiritual encounter in what they write and never belittle anything a child has written. Remember that when a child shares any deep inner spiritual experience, their capacity to express it remains limited by their cognitive development and language skills, so their descriptions may seem not to be related to God, even though it may well be an experience of the real presence. Parents and teachers then need to listen carefully, very attentively to what is really being said, especially where the truth of the experience is ultimately inexpressible. One needs to remember, as we explored earlier, that the word is not the thing; it is merely an inadequate means of pointing towards an indescribable truth, a stepping stone toward an ineffable reality that can nonetheless be intuited and experienced.

The purpose of the exercise is not to convince children about anything but to engage them in easy conversation about aspects of their experience that they may not have considered before and to help them honour the potential depth of meaning of their experience.

Using the Selection Box to Generate Conversation about Meditation

As part of my research I devised a simple, tactile method that allowed each child, during their second-round interview, to respond to comments other children had made. The comments were brief statements such as 'Meditation helps me to be calm and relaxed' or 'Meditation helps me to be myself'. The comments were typed onto paper and cut into rectangles, roughly the size of a credit card, and laminated. The cards were left in a pile and each child was asked to pick them up and to go through them one by one, at their own pace, handle each comment physically and respond tacitly, non-verbally, by distinguishing between those comments which resonated with them and those that did not.

Also on the table was a closed box. It was a cardboard box, with a pull-out drawer with had two divisions, yes and no. When the drawer was opened, the child saw that the word 'yes' was written in green lettering in the left-hand section and the word 'no' in red on the right. As the child read each card, they were asked to place it in the 'yes' box if they too had experienced what they understood it to say, in the 'no' box if it didn't resonate with their own experience and on top of the box if they were unsure or if they did not know what the comment meant. I have called this method the Selection Box.[6] When they had finished the exercise, which was conducted in silence, we began to talk about the comments they had chosen. Lesson five incorporates a variation of this method.

Lesson Five | Generating Conversation about Meditation through the Selection Box

Aim: To generate conversation with the children about meditation as a spiritual practice and to explore the spiritual fruits of meditation.

Learning Outcomes: Children will make connections regarding the spiritual fruits of meditation or will hear how other children did so.

Key Elements

- Presenting children with a series of comments made by other children about meditation.
- Facilitating a sensitive discussion with those children who wish to contribute on meditation as a spiritual practice.

1. Listed here, in no particular order, are comments that any teacher or parent can use to generate discussion with children. Simply explain that other children have said these things about meditation and you wonder if they mean anything to your children.
   - Meditation helps me to get things off my mind.
   - Meditation helps me to feel a sense of freedom.
   - Meditation helps me to be more aware of the goodness in myself.
   - Meditation helps me to know that I am loved.
   - Meditation helps me to find the real me.

- Meditation helps me to open my heart.
- Meditation helps me to be a happier person.
- Meditation helps me to feel God's love.
- Meditation helps me to get on better with others.
- Meditation helps me be calm and relaxed.
- Meditation helps me to be close to Jesus.
- Meditation helps me to be a nicer person.
- Meditation helps me to discover things about myself.
- Meditation helps me to connect with God.
- Meditation helps me to make better decisions.
- Meditation helps me to be myself.
- Meditation helps me to see the goodness in others.
- Meditation helps me to be grateful.
- Meditation helps me to accept myself as I am.
- Meditation helps me to do better in school.

Invite each child to pick one or two comments that mean something special to them based on their own experience of meditation. Ask them to write a few sentences about what their chosen comment meant to them, saying why they chose it and these can be collected by the teacher. The teacher could use what the children have written anonymously at a later date to summarise sensitively the key fruits mentioned by the children in the class (without revealing any details that could identify any child) and the summary could be used to generate a discussion on the subject. Instead of using all twenty comments at the one time, a small selection might be shown and the remainder used on other occasions, enabling you to return to the question perhaps once per school term.

An alternative way of doing this exercise is to use the posters produced by the Meditation with Children project.[7] Each poster contains an image of a child or children meditating and each has a simple phrase describing a fruit of meditation in language used by the children. I should stress that the phrases on each poster were not those of the child depicted in the poster – the images of children who had agreed to be photographed were randomly matched with the phrases that emerged from the research.

You might engage with children along the following lines, saying something like, 'This poster says "Meditation Helps You Be Yourself". When children were asked how meditation helped them, that's what many of them said. I wonder what they meant by that? We started meditating in this classroom about [number of weeks or months] ago. So, all of you have been meditating for some time now. In what way do you think meditation helps you to be yourself?'

Another poster features a boy wearing a hoodie with the words 'MM Monkey Mind'. You could show this poster and ask what is written on the front of the boy's hoodie. The phrase 'monkey mind' is sometimes used to describe how busy the mind gets, how it constantly jumps from one thought to the next just like a monkey jumps from branch to branch, over and over again without any clear purpose. It was pure chance that he happened to be wearing a hoodie bearing that message on the day the image was taken. Talk with the children about what it is like to have a 'monkey mind' and ask them to describe how meditation helps to calm down the mind.

The wording on another poster reads 'Meditation Awakens the Heart'. You might ask the children what they think the child who said this meant. Stress that you don't want them to guess, you only want them to answer if it reminds them of something they too may have experienced in meditation or as a fruit of meditation. Everybody is different and the experience of each child will be personal and unique. You may find there are several children for whom that phrase rings a bell, but they have different interpretations – in other words, the phrase was meaningful to each of them but not in exactly the same way. It is important to stress that there are no right or wrong answers. It's like asking someone their favourite food: everyone will have their own answer and every one of them is right.

Being Authentic: Living the Fruits Every Day

It is important that when one speaks with children about meditation that one does so with authenticity. Very real benefits and deep inner fruits flow from the practice of meditation; however, they do not arise simply by reading about meditation. The benefits and fruits flow from daily, or at least regular, meditation practice.

One can understand meditation conceptually and that will enable you to explain it, but you will be able to speak about it all the more authentically if you practise meditation yourself. Then you will know both conceptually and perceptually that meditation does indeed lead to deep inner and outer flourishing. Then the fruits of meditation move from a theoretical abstraction to a practical manifestation and you become the change you want to see in the world.

While your words are very important and you must choose them very carefully when relating to children, it is how you are more than what you say that is important. Children, like adults, recognise and honour authenticity and dislike inauthenticity. So, an adult teaching meditation to children must have developed their own self-awareness and authenticity to a high degree. Maya Angelou once observed that people will forget what you said, people will forget what you did, but people will never forget how you made them feel.

Let me give a very practical example. Recently, I visited a classroom in a school that had adopted meditation as a whole-school practice and it was immediately obvious that the teacher had an excellent relationship with the children. She had engaged with them at the start of the school year about their expectations. She had asked them to say how they would like to be treated by one another and by her so that they would have a comfortable and safe environment in their classroom, so that everyone could feel they belonged. Each 'wish' was captured in a speech bubble and added to a special notice board. She regularly referred to it, especially when the children were being their best selves; and occasionally to draw attention to a behaviour she observed that hadn't lived up to the values of their special board. This was never done crossly, but gently and lovingly, reminding the children of how they had said they wished to be together. In attempting to hold to those aspirations, the children were not driven by a sense of duty but by a deeper sense of who they truly were. They represented their desire to live authentically.

Parents and teachers can point out to children the connections between living well and meditation. For example, in meditation the intention is to be still in body and mind, to be still in God's presence. To help us achieve that, every time we find we have gotten caught up in a thought, we gently let go of it and return to our sacred word. Meditation is about starting over and over again. It is about returning to our intention, forgetting about it, realising that we have forgotten it and yielded to another thought, and returning once again to repeating our word. Life is like that too. We intend to live and behave in one way, yet we often fail to measure up and we behave in ways of which we are not proud. That happens because we fall out of self-awareness as we get caught up in our conditioning, out thoughts, our worries, our desires.

As noted in chapter two, it seems as if our self-awareness has a dimmer switch that automatically dims as we allow our attention to become fragmented by our incessant distractions. But meditation builds up our 'attention muscle', as we consciously return again and again to our intention to sit in stillness and silence. Meditation teaches us that all we have to do is pick ourselves up and start again. And because we are in the habit of doing that over and over again in meditation, it becomes easier to do it at other times as well – to return to our intention to be our best selves and to live authentically in the present moment. Likewise, because meditation improves self-awareness, we notice more easily what is happening, how we are behaving in the present moment, not just afterwards, but as we do it and we develop a greater capacity to change what we were about to do so that it becomes responsive not reactive, so that our actions are genuinely appropriate to the circumstances. We learn to ask ourselves, even under pressure, 'What is the most loving response I can make in this situation?'

What was remarkable about this teacher was her capacity to be clear and open about what she expected from herself and to hold herself to account also. She made it clear to the children that she would always try to live out the values of the affirmation board and that when she failed she too would acknowledge it and start again. I think that was a vital part of her relationship with them. Because she was willing to be authentic with them, they found it easier to be authentic with her and with their classmates. This teacher mentioned that if she is finding it difficult to manage things in the classroom, if she notices that she is getting a little bit stressed, she will sometimes say to the children that she feels she is getting a little bit cross and she will ask if they can all take some time out to meditate for just a minute. Of course, it was probably no surprise to the children; the likelihood is that they saw her 'crossness' emerging even before she did. But, she said, they always responded very well to her request and they would all meditate in silence for a minute or two. And she, and they, were always the better for having done so.

The fruits of meditation will be manifest in the lives of the meditator. It will be visible in the way a teacher relates to their class, in the way a parent relates to their children and spouse. Ultimately, values are caught, not taught. As the old verse says, 'No printed word nor spoken plea will inspire young hearts what they can be, not all the books on all the shelves, but what the teachers are themselves.' While meditation will develop children's self-awareness, awaken their hearts to the true-self, nourish their spirituality and inspire authentic living, they also need to experience in their daily lives living exemplars of what it means to live authentically.

Practice Seven

Now that you have a better understanding of what it means to meditate, why not set the timer on your phone for fifteen minutes and enjoy a fifteen-minute meditation.

Follow the instructions in practice two (page 62) but this time extend your period of meditation to fifteen minutes.

Endnotes

1. Cathy Ota, 'The Conflict between Pedagogical Effectiveness and Spiritual Development in Catholic Schools' in Jane Erricker, Cathy Ota and Clive Erricker (eds), *Spiritual Education: Cultural, Religious and Social Differences: New Perspectives for the 21st Century*, Eastbourne, UK: Sussex Academic Press 2001, p. 271.

2. The quote was made by Dr Kate Adams in a paper for the British Educational Research Association in 2009. See Christopher Lamb, 'Children's spiritual needs neglected' *The Tablet*, 5 September 2009, p. 36.

3. Mata, who researched how four kindergarten children experienced and expressed spirituality, challenged Tobin Hart's depiction of children's spiritual lives as 'secret spiritual lives'. The difference may well be a function of age. However, in Mata's case, she was not attending to how children communicated with one another and the significant adults in their lives about their spirituality, rather she focused on how their innate spirituality found expression in their ordinary daily lives, expressions to which adults may have been insensitive.

4. A selection of images is available on the Meditation and Children page at: www.christianmeditation.ie.

5. If any child considers that none of the images relates to their experience, they might be asked instead to write a few sentences to say what they liked or disliked about meditation and whether they considered it helped them in any way.

6. For further information, Noel Keating, 'Children's Spirituality and the Practice of Meditation in Irish Primary Schools', *International Journal for Children's Spirituality*, 22(1), 2017, pp. 49–71.

7. These are available on the website www.christianmeditation.ie and may be downloaded.

Concluding Remarks

Throughout this book I have explored the child's experience of meditation, the nature of children's spirituality and the impact meditation can have in nurturing their spirituality. I drew on learning from across a range of disciplines and from my own doctoral research. By way of conclusion, I would like to draw together some of the book's key insights.

Firstly, it is widely accepted that children have an innate capacity for spirituality that can be experienced by them as deeply meaningful; however, they may not have the cognitive or language capacity to give rational and coherent verbal expression to it. Spirituality may be understood in secular terms as an inner dynamism that guides the human person towards fullness of life. It may be described in religious terms for people of faith as a search for the true-self, for communion with the divine and a willingness to live life from that perspective. In any case, spiritual experience normally has an ordinary everyday quality about it – it is not generally experienced as extraordinary but expresses itself in moments of wonder, awe and joy and is manifest in the search for meaning and purpose in life.

Secondly, the children who participated in my research loved to meditate and enjoyed doing so on a whole-school basis and at home. They found that, over time, it gave rise to practical, pragmatic benefits and deep inner fruits. These chapters give voice to the child's experience of meditation, to their unique expression of how they experience meditation and its benefits and fruits in their lives. While previous research had given an account of how children benefitted from the practice of meditation, this book gives a clear account of how they experience its spiritual fruits also. They described the experience of meditation as being simple and serene and as giving rise to greater self-awareness and deep heart-awareness. Meditation enabled them to let go of stress, it calmed and restored them, it generated energy and confidence in them and it helped them to make better decisions. Regarding the fruits of meditation, chapter four demonstrated how meaningful the children found the practice and it contained many insightful expressions of how they had experienced its deep inner fruits. They found it helped them to be themselves, to be true to themselves and to be deeply consciousness of the goodness within themselves and every other person. They are capable of and do enjoy personal spiritual experience through the practice. Meditation brought them closer God, to the creative life force that transcends them, and it made them kinder as people. To express it succinctly, meditation has the capacity to transform their way of seeing and being in the world. Many children said they became more responsive and less reactive, indicating that meditation guided them somehow to live more authentic lives. The children's accounts also reveal how meditation has the capacity to build community. I am not suggesting, however, that every child who meditates will experience all of the benefits and fruits but that the regular practice of meditation leaves them open to receiving them.

Concluding Remarks

The spread of secular mindfulness meditation across the world in recent decades is to be welcomed by all, including people of faith. Meditation surpasses the boundaries of religion and culture – it is a universal practice that finds unique expression across different cultures. These various forms differ in particular in their intention and in how they describe its deeper fruits; however, they all point to the capacity of meditation to promote human flourishing with consequent benefits for society, when it is practised regularly and faithfully. The theistic religions of the world, including Christianity, go further, pointing to the integration of the body, mind and spirit and the transformation of the person. As I have described it, meditation changes our way of seeing and being in the world. In Christian terms, our lives become ever more Christ-centred, not merely in a pious way, but on the very practical level indicated by the parable of the Good Samaritan.

Meditation is often introduced in a secular context for its benefits and in a faith context for its spiritual fruits. But, even when it is introduced in a purely secular context it will be helpful, for the sake of completeness, to point out that many people adopt meditation as a spiritual practice because of its fruits and to name how those traditions describe its fruits. In other words, it is desirable, even in a secular context, that children have information about the diverse perspectives different traditions bring to the practice. Laurence Freeman suggests that those who incorporate meditation practice as part of their secular lifestyle may in time be 'surprised by joy' and may eventually awaken to the spiritual fruits of the practice. In such circumstances, meditation may give rise to the first stages of a spiritual journey of faith.[1] Ultimately, each child will find meaning in their own experience of the practice, in light of their family and cultural norms.

For people of faith, meditation can be a bridge to an ever-deepening spirituality and it can lead to the discovery of the true-self. In the silence of the present moment they are able to apprehend reality as it truly is. Over time silence becomes a living language of encounter with the divine, which informs how they live. This book demonstrates that childhood is a very fertile ground for spirituality and that children experience spirituality as profoundly relational. As Karl Rahner observed, children are fundamentally oriented toward God and their spirituality arises from within, from their own existence and experience. Of course, there are many portals to spiritual experience and one needs a balanced approach to prayer. But this book argues that the Western Churches have tended towards an imbalance in favour of discursive (kataphatic) prayer – prayer involving words and images. This imbalance can, and should, be addressed by promoting practices such as meditation in the school, home and parish. A significant number of the children in my study meditated at home as well as in school. Indeed, several had introduced their parents to meditation or had begun to meditate with parents who were already familiar with the practice. This creates real opportunities for families to meditate together and can lead to the renewal of a spiritual dimension in family life.

This book stresses the vital importance of ensuring that children have access to opportunities to engage their own spirituality and to recognise and value it. Meditation has very rich potential for enabling children to do so. Hence, it is important to provide children with opportunities for meditation, ideally in the home, parish and school so they come to realise it is truly a gift for life. Meditation can be practised anywhere, at any time, on one's own or in a group or community setting. It is noted in chapter three that many studies suggest that in Western culture, as children pass the age of eight or nine, their innate spiritual potential begins to be repressed by the dominant secular norms of modern society. In light of my approach to defining spirituality, I suggest that this dis-ease of the modern world might be called 'true-self-denial'. This book suggests that meditation has the capacity to counter true-self-denial, enabling children to discover their true-selves below the surface of their everyday awareness, and to recognise and honour their true nature, the whole of their being and to trust in the integrity of perceptual, spiritual knowledge. One of the difficulties faced by teachers and parents is that it is not easy to see into children's spiritual lives. This calls for teachers to explore their own understanding and experience of spirituality and to learn about children's spirituality. I hope this book makes a small contribution in that direction.

As well as providing a simple introduction to meditation, the book is a practical resource for teachers and parents. The lessons in chapters five and six offer a simple method for introducing the practice to children and young people. The approach taken – first introducing meditation as a holistic practice that promotes well-being, then outlining the benefits in some detail and finally exploring what the traditions say about its deeper, spiritual fruits – builds on the children's personal capacity, on their power within, on what the child already has rather than adding something new. It stresses the primacy of personal spiritual experience as a pathway to spiritual growth. In a faith-based setting it is vital that all three lessons are covered over time so that the children will have a basis for understanding the inner spaciousness and energy that arises from the practice and have an understanding of how the practice relates to their faith tradition and its approach to prayer as loving communion with God.

This approach, outlined in the first three lessons, can work successfully in both a secular and a faith context. In a secular context, lesson three can be presented as information about faith traditions – what they say about the spiritual fruits of meditation. In a faith context, parents, parishes and faith schools can present it in terms of faith-formation and explore more deeply the intention of the practice in their faith tradition and the language used in their tradition to describe the spiritual fruits. Meditation can provide a very receptive ground for faith. It can help practitioners, including children, to experience, understand and verify the essential truths of their faith – as distinct from its beliefs – in light of their personal spiritual experience. Meditation can provide a very solid basis for inter-religious dialogue also, for developing a shared understanding of the human person as innately spiritual. Christianity would do well to embrace the opportunity created by the spread of secular mindfulness and engage in dialogue with the modern world as urged by the Second Vatican Council:

Carried out with prudence and love and in witness to the Christian faith and life, we are called to recognise, preserve and promote the good things, spiritual and moral, as well as the socio-cultural values found among different practices.[2]

Meditation can also help to create intergenerational dialogue about the meaning of spirituality, the ways in which people in a secular society can strive to live authentic lives and the capacity of community to provide invaluable support in doing so. The practice of meditation can build community within and across faith traditions and secular society.

Ultimately, meditation leads to the discovery of the true-self, whether that is described in religious or secular, humanist language. I urge the reader to try it and see for yourself; discover for yourself that, as Jason (12) said, 'Meditation is like a map and the destination is who you really are.'

Endnotes

1. Laurence Freeman, *The Contemplative Dimension of the New Evangelisation: Christian Meditation in the Church in a Secular World*, World Community for Christian Meditation: ISSUU, 2015.

2. Vatican, 'Nostrae Aetate (1965)' in Austin Flannery (ed.), *Vatican Council II: Constitutions, Decrees, Declarations: The Basic Sixteen Documents*, Dublin Dominican Publications, 1996, p. 571.

Epilogue

I began this book by pointing out what inspired me to undertake this journey. My personal experience of meditation deepened my awareness of my true-self and transfigured my way of seeing and being in the world. While I was pleased to see the practice of mindfulness introduced to schools for its practical benefits, I was concerned that children were not being alerted to the deep spiritual fruits of meditation. The more I have researched and written about the practice of meditation with children, the more I realise the importance of personal spiritual experience on our journey towards spiritual maturity. As Willigis Jäger expresses it, 'Something happens to the person at prayer ... Something happens to the pray-er. It is an awakening to one's true divine essence.'[1] The practice of meditation deepens one's awareness of the true nature of the human person, of the true-self. The timeless nature of this truth, of this deep personal conviction, is captured beautifully in the following verse by Rainer Maria Rilke:

> A billion stars go spinning through the night,
> Blazing high above your head.
> But in you is the presence that will be,
> When all the stars are dead.[2]

Thomas Merton also penned some lines which poetically capture that same truth:

Meditation with Children

There is in all visible things an invisible fecundity, a dimmed light, a meek namelessness, a hidden wholeness ... There is in all things an inexhaustible sweetness and purity, a silence that is a fount of action and joy. It rises up in wordless gentleness and flows out to me from the unseen roots of all created being, welcoming me tenderly, saluting me with indescribable humility.[3]

I urge parents, teachers and school principals, and parishes to find the courage to begin. While the practice is simple, it isn't easy. But it is very easy to begin – all it requires is willingness to give it a go. Meditation does not require a high level of education – there is more than enough information in this book. It does not require much by way of resources – at its simplest level all that is required is a timer, but resources are widely available.[4] This book adds to the resources available, providing an insight, in the words of children themselves, into their experience of meditation and its fruits. Its accessible lesson plans provide a simple means of introducing the practice to children and engaging with them about their experience.

Endnotes

1. Willigis Jäger, *Search for the Meaning of Life: Essays and Reflections of the Mystical Experience*, Ligouri, Missouri: Liguori/Triumph, 2003, Kindle location 1414 of 5436.

2. Rainer Maria Rilke, 'Buddha in Glory' in *Ahead of All Parting: The Selected Poetry and Prose of Rainer Maria Rilke*, New York: Random House, 1995, p. 75.

3. Thomas Merton, 'Hagia Sophia: Dawn' in Lynn R. Szabo (ed.), *In the Dark before Dawn: New Selected Poems of Thomas Merton*, New York: New Directions, 2005, p. 65.

4. The Meditation with Children project in Ireland (www.christianmeditation.ie) offers resources for free, including meditation tracks, which are accessible and downloadable from anywhere. The website also contains a list of meditation groups across Ireland. The website of the world community (wccm.org) does likewise for communities across the globe and contains many other resources.

Grounding Prayer

Abba Father, open my heart
So your Word may find a home in me.
Jesus Lord, I am blind,
Make me aware that I may see.
Holy Spirit, awaken me,
So as you wish, I may be.

Appendix One | Secular Mindfulness and Christian Meditation Compared

ASPECT	SECULAR MINDFULNESS	CHRISTIAN MEDITATION
NATURE	A Secular Practice	A Spiritual Practice
FORM	Open-Monitoring Meditation • Focus on the breath • Detached observation of thoughts, feelings and emotions arising Grounded in stillness and silence	Focused-Attention Meditation • Focus on a sacred word • Acknowledgement and letting go of thoughts, feelings and emotions arising Letting go who you are not Grounded in stillness and silence
FREQUENCY	Twice daily for 20–30 minutes	Twice daily for 20–30 minutes
INTENTION	Person-centred Being, not doing Dwelling in the present moment as it is without desiring to change it	God-centred/Christ-centred; a silent, wordless, imageless form of prayer Being, not doing Dwelling in the present moment, where God is present, without desiring to change it

Figure 7.1: Secular Mindfulness and Christian Meditation Compared (continued on next page)

(continued from previous page)

INTENTION	Oriented towards practical benefits	Oriented towards spiritual fruits
		Benefits seen to arise as a welcome but incidental by-product
PERCEIVED OUTCOMES	Practical benefits include:	Practical benefits include:
	Improved well-being in terms of physical, mental, cognitive and emotional health	Improved well-being in terms of physical, mental, cognitive and emotional health
	Greater self-awareness and self-acceptance and an improved sense of wholeness. Promotion of the integration of the person physically and psychologically	Spiritual fruits include: A transformed sense of self-identity Knowledge of the true-self Awareness of real presence Integration of mind, body and spirit
	Promotion of an attitude of compassion and loving kindness towards others	A new way of seeing and being in the world
		Greater clarity of perception More responsive than reactive More authentic, compassionate living
		The fruits of the Spirit are described in scripture as love, joy, peace, patience, kindness, goodness, faithfulness, gentleness, and self-control (Gal 5:22–3)

Figure 7.1: Secular Mindfulness and Christian Meditation Compared

Appendix Two | What Teachers Said

As part of my research, I interviewed the teachers of each class from which children volunteered to be interviewed, as well as the school principals and, where one had been appointed, coordinators of the Meditation with Children project. There was a consensus that the practice was beneficial to the children and the school, particularly in terms of mental health. As Brian expressed it, 'It definitely makes a contribution to the life of the school, to the atmosphere in the class, to the attitude of the children and it focuses them.' Siobhan, the coordinator of the practice in one of the schools, considered that while the children may 'not realise that they are benefitting, they will realise [it] as they get older. They are getting something from it, perhaps without fully knowing.' Deirdre, a teacher from the same school, saw meditation as an important life skill, 'We are equipping these young minds to be able to exercise control over how they react to situations ... [to] exercise [more control] over their lives ... I see the meditation as a really important part of that.' Aoife felt that 'this generation probably needs meditation more than any previous generation'. Bernie observed that the children could just be themselves in meditation: 'I just get the greatest joy out of watching the faces of the ones that really are into it because they are striving all the time to be so grown up, to be so super cool, to be what everybody else thinks they should be. By contrast, you see the absolute innocence of their faces when they are being themselves in meditation.'

Meditation with Children

Amber was one of a number of teachers who noted how children with special needs, including those diagnosed with ASD (autistic spectrum disorder), benefitted from the practice. Several teachers noted that meditation especially helped children who exhibited emotional or anger issues. Deirdre recalled one child in particular who often found himself in conflict with his mother and who discovered that meditating at home had really helped to resolve it. She often observed his embodied tension dissolve during meditation in class, 'It was like seeing a knot being undone, so that after meditation he was able to participate better in class.' Rachel, however, found that those children who 'need most to shut out their worries' were the ones who were initially least disposed to meditation, but they had settled in to it over time and benefited from it.

Bernie commented that she found meditation very helpful in her own life. She had a tendency to overthink things and to worry a lot but she found that after meditation she would notice 'the tension, kind of just seeping out of [me], which surprised me. I was astonished that it was so simple and yet so effective.' A new teacher to the school, Bernie had never practised meditation with children and was inclined to think it would be a waste of precious teaching time, but, having implemented it over her first year in her new school, she now understands its value and would not want to see the practice cease. She found the children were calmer and more focused after meditation.

Caitriona sometimes gave the children an opportunity to comment on their experience after meditation. She recalls 'being stunned by some of what they said, about how it made them feel. How when they opened their eyes after meditation, the world seemed brighter. If I had needed any convincing that there were benefits to doing this, in my own life, I got it from them because of what they were saying.' Teachers spoke of the grounding impact of meditation and many considered that immediately after yard-time following lunch was a good time for meditation because it grounds the children for the final part of the school day.

Just like the children, many of the teachers valued the fact that silence extended over the whole school at the same time and not just their own classroom alone.

Appendix Three | Sustaining Meditation Practice in a School

It was very clear from the conversations with the teachers, principals and coordinators that while the practice was straightforward and easy to introduce, it did require ongoing attention and energy to sustain it. Schools are very dynamic places; curriculum change is frequent and new initiatives are regularly imposed. It can happen that the latest initiative, accompanied by in-service training and sometimes subject to inspection, can draw attention away from previous initiatives. A great deal depends on the professionalism of the principal and the senior management team.

In the longer term, for the project to become embedded in a school, it seems that a number of factors make a vibrant contribution to its sustainability:

- The commitment of the principal to any initiative is vital to its success. The Meditation with Children project flourishes in schools where the principal understands the deep value of the practice and ensures that it is a regular focus of discussion with teachers. In addition, principals can ensure that meditation is an integral part of school assemblies, in a way that speaks to and honours its spiritual fruits.

- Several principals appointed a named member of staff to coordinate the project and that too proved to be very helpful in sustaining meditation as a whole-school practice. It helps also where the principal and/or the meditation coordinator visits classes from time to time specifically to meditate with different class groups and to speak with them about it.

- Starting staff meetings with a short meditation is another powerful and meaningful way of reinforcing the value of the practice.

- Many teachers took care to make explicit links between elements of the RE programme and the practice of meditation. Ideally, the school's spiritual development and religious education policy will refer to the fact that meditation is an integral part of the life of the faith community of the school.

- The appointment of a small team to support and review the practice is also very helpful. As well as signifying that the practice is sufficiently important to warrant a support team, it creates a process whereby the practice can be regularly referred to and reviewed. It keeps the spotlight on the practice and can lead to some very fruitful exchanges across the staff.

- Once the practice has been introduced and is embedded in the life of the school, it is important that it does not become just 'another thing we do every day' or every few days. Teachers need to spend some time, ideally once a month, returning to some aspect or other of the practice to remind the children of their intention in meditation and of its deep spiritual fruits.

Bibliography

Benson, Herbert, *Beyond the Relaxation Response*, New York: Berkley Books, 1984. *The Relaxation Response*, New York: HarperTorch, 1975.

Berryman, Jerome W., 'Silence is stranger than it used to be: Teaching silence and the future of humankind' in Brendan Hyde (ed.), *The Search for a Theology of Childhood: Essays by Jerome W. Berryman from 1978–2009*, Ballarat, Victoria: Modotti Press, 2013.

Bourgeault, Cynthia, *The Heart of Centering Prayer: Nondual Christianity in Theory and Practice*, Boulder, CO: Shambala, 2016.

Browning, Robert, 'Paracelsus' in D.H.S Nicholson and A.H.E. Lee (eds), *The Oxford Book of English Mystical Verse*, Oxford: Clarendon Press, 1917.

Butcher, Carmen Acevedo, *Cloud of Unknowing: With the Book of Privy Council: A New Translation*, London: Shambhala, 2011.

Buttle, Heather, 'Measuring a Journey without Goal: Meditation, Spirituality, and Physiology', *BioMed Research International*, 2015.

Campion, Jonathan, 'A Review of the Research on Meditation', *The Meditation Journal: Education*, 1(1), 2011, pp. 29–37.

Campion, Jonathan, and Rocco, Sharn, 'Minding the Mind: The Effects and Potential of a School-Based Meditation Programme for Mental Health Promotion', *Advances in School Mental Health Promotion*, 2(1), 2009, pp. 47–55.

Cavalletti, Sofia, *The Religious Potential of the Child: The Description of an Experience with Children from Ages Three to Six*, The Missionary Society of St Paul the Apostle (trans.), New York: Paulist Press, 1983.

Chessick, Richard D., 'Heidegger's Narcissism and His Philosophy' in *Mimetic Desire: Essays on Narcissism in German Literature from Romanticism to Postmodernism (Studies in German Literature Linguistics and Culture)*, Jeffrey Adams and Eric Williams (eds), Columbia, SC: Camden House, 1995, pp. 103–18.

Christie, Ernie. *Coming Home: A Guide to Teaching Christian Meditation to Children*. Singapore: Medio Media, 2008.

Coles, Robert, *The Spiritual Life of Children*. London: HarperCollins, 1992.

Crescentini, Cristiano, Viviana Capurso, Samantha Furlan, and Franco Fabbro, 'Mindfulness-Oriented Meditation for Primary School Children:

Effects on Attention and Psychological Well-Being', *Frontiers in Psychology*, 2016.

Culliford, Larry, *The Psychology of Spirituality: An Introduction*, London: Jessica Kingsley Publishers, 2011.

de Mello, Anthony, *One Minute Nonsense*, Anand, India: Gujarat Sahitya Prakash, 1992.

————, *One Minute Wisdom*, Anand, India: Gujarat Sahitya Prakash, 1985.

de Wit, Han F., 'The Case for Contemplative Psychology', *Shambhala Sun*, March 2001.

————, *Contemplative Psychology*, Marie Louise Baird (trans.), Pittsburgh, PA: Dubuesne University Press, 1991, p. 10.

————, 'On Contemplative Psychology', paper presented at the Third Symposium on the Psychology of Religion in Europe, Amsterdam, 1986.

————, 'On the Methodology of Clarifying Confusion' in *Current Issues in Theoretical Psychology*, William J. Baker, Michael E. Hyland, Hans Van Rappard and Arthur W. Staats (eds), Amsterdam: Elsevier Science Publishers B.V., 1987.

————, *The Spiritual Path: An Introduction to the Psychology of the Spiritual Traditions*, Henry Jansen and Lucia Hofland-Jensen (trans), Pittsburgh, PA: Duquense University Press, 1999.

Dresler, Martin, Anders Sandberg, Kathrin Ohla, Christoph Bublitz, Carlos Trenado, Aleksandra Mroczko-Wasowicz, Simone Kühn, and Dimitris Repantis, 'Non-Pharmacological Cognitive Enhancement', *Neuropharmacology* 64 (2013), pp. 529–43. Accessed 12 April 2017, dx.doi.org/10.1016/j.neuropharm.2012.07.002

Eckhart, Meister, 'Sermon on the Fourth Sunday after Trinity', James M. Clark and John V. Skinner (trans) in *Meister Eckhart: Selected Treatises and Sermons*, London: Faber and Faber, 1958.

Everly, George S. and Jeffrey Lating, M., *A Clinical Guide to the Treatment of Human Stress Response*, New York: Springer, 2013.

Finley, James, *Christian Meditation: Experiencing the Presence of God*, New York: HarperCollins, 2004.

Finnegan, Jack, *The Audacity of Spirit: The Meaning and Shaping of Spirituality Today*, Dublin: Veritas, 2008.

Flanagan, Bernadette, 'Christian Spirituality and Religious Mysticism: Adjunct, Parallel or Embedded Concepts?' in *Spirituality Across*

Disciplines: Research and Practice, Marian de Souza, Jane Bone and Jacqueline Watson (eds), Cham, Switzerland: Springer International Publishing, 2016.

Freeman, Laurence, 'The Contemplative Dimension of the New Evangelisation: Christian Meditation in the Church in a Secular World', World Community for Christian Meditation: ISSUU, 2015.

——, *Health and Wholeness*, London: World Community for Christian Meditation, 2015.

——, 'Jesus' in Kim Nataraja (ed.), *Journey to the Heart: Christian Contemplation through the Centuries – an Illustrated Guide*, London: Canterbury Press, 2011.

——, *Jesus: The Teacher Within*, Norwich: SCM Press, 2010.

——, 'A Letter from Laurence Freeman', *Christian Meditation Newsletter*, 33(4), 2009.

——, *Your Daily Practice*, Singapore: Medio Media, 2008.

Frost, Robert, *A Witness Tree*, New York: Henry Holt & Co., 1942.

Gallacher, Patrick J. (ed.), *The Cloud of Unknowing*, Teams Middle English Text Series Kalamazoo, Mich: Western Michigan University Medieval Institute Publications, 1997.

Goleman, Daniel, *The Meditative Mind: The Varieties of Meditative Experience*, Digital ed., Florence, MA: More Than Sound, 2012.

Green, Jim, *The Heart of Education: Meditation with Children and Young People*, London: Meditatio – World Community for Christian Meditation, 2016.

Hanh, Thich Nhat, *Interbeing: Commentaries on the Tiep Hien Precepts*, Delhi: Full Circle Publishing, 2003.

Harris, Paul, 'John Main and the Practice of Christian Meditation', www.bahaistudies.net/asma/johnmain.pdf

Hart, Tobin, *The Secret Spiritual World of Children*, Novato, CA: New World Library, 2003.

Hay, David and Rebecca Nye, *The Spirit of the Child*, Revised ed., London: Jessica Kingsley Publishers, 1998.

Hennelly, Sarah, 'The immediate and sustained effects of the .b mindfulness programme on adolescents' social and emotional well-being and academic functioning', Oxford Brookes University, 2011.

Hinsdale, Mary Ann, '"Infinite Openness to the Infinite": Karl Rahner's

Contribution to Modern Catholic Thought on the Child' in Marcia J. Bunge (ed.), *The Child in Christian Thought*, Grand Rapids, Michigan: Wm. B. Eerdmans Publishing Co., 2001, pp. 406–45.

Hove, Philo, 'Learning Retreat Meditation' in Max van Manen (ed.) *Writing in the Dark: Phenomenological Studies in Interpretive Inquiry*, Walnut Creek, CA: Left Coast Press, 2015, pp. 197–220.

Jäger, Willigis, *Search for the Meaning of Life: Essays and Reflections of the Mystical Experience*, Ligouri, Missouri: Liguori/Triumph, 2003.

Kabat-Zinn, Jon, *Full Catastrophe Living: Using the Wisdom of Your Body and Mind to Face Stress, Pain and Illness*, New York: Bantam Books, 2013, 1990.

———, *Mindfulness for Beginners: Reclaiming the Present Moment – and Your Life*, Boulder, CO: Sounds True, 2012.

———, 'Mindfulness Meditation: What It Is, What It Isn't, and Its Role in Health Care and Medicine' in Y. Haruki, Y. Ishii, and M. Suzuki (eds), *Comparative and Psychological Study on Meditation*, Netherlands: Eburon, 1996.

Kavanagh, Patrick, 'Having Confessed' in *Collected Poems*, W.W. Norton & Company, 2004.

Keating, Noel, 'Children's Spirituality and the Practice of Meditation in Irish Primary Schools', *International Journal for Children's Spirituality*, 22(1), 2017, pp. 49–71.

Keating, Thomas, Open Mind, Open Heart: The Contemplative Dimension of the Gospel, New Your: Continuum, 2003.

Kornfield, Jack, *Meditation for Beginners*, Boulder, Colorado: Sounds True, 2004.

Louchakova-Schwartz, Olga, 'Cognitive Phenomenology in the Study of Tibetan Meditation: Phenomenological Descriptions Versus Meditation Styles' in Susan Gordan (ed.), *Neurophenomenology and Its Applications to Psychology*, New York: Springer Science and Business Media, 2013.

Lustyk, M.K. et al., 'Mindfulness Meditation Research: Issues of Participant Screening, Safety Procedures, and Researcher Training', *Advances in Mind-Body Medicine*, 24(1), 2009, pp. 20–30.

Main, John, *Community of Love*, Singapore: Medio Media, 2010.

———, *The Hunger for Depth and Meaning: Learning to Meditate with John Main*, Singapore: Medio Media, 2007.

———, *In Times of Anxiety*, London: The World Community for Christian Meditation, 2009.

Bibliography

————, *Moment of Christ: The Path of Meditation*, London: Bloomsbury, 1998.

————, *Our Hearts Burned within Us: Reading the New Testament with John Main*, Singapore: Medio Media, 2012.

————, *Word into Silence: A Manual for Christian Meditation*, Norwich: Canterbury Press, 2006.

May, Gerald, *Will and Spirit: A Contemplative Psychology*, New York: HarperCollins, 1987.

McGinn, Bernard, *The Foundations of Mysticism: Origins to the Fifth Century*, New York: Crossroad, 1991.

Merton, Thomas, 'Hagia Sophia: Dawn' in *In the Dark before Dawn: New Selected Poems of Thomas Merton*, Lynn R. Szabo (ed.), New York: New Directions, 2005.

————, *New Seeds of Contemplation*, New York: A New Dirctions Book, 1961.

————, *The Wisdom of the Desert: Sayings from the Desert Fathers of the Fourth Century*, New York: A New Directions Book, 1961.

————, *Zen and the Birds of Appetite*, New York: New Directions Publishing, 1968.

Nataraja, Shanida, *The Blissful Brain: Neuroscience and Proof of the Power of Meditation*, London: Octopus Publishing, 2008.

————, *Revised and Updated: The Blissful Brain: Neuroscience and Proof of the Power of Meditation*, London (Amazon Kindle Edition): Dr Shanida Nataraja, 2014.

Nye, Rebecca, *Children's Spirituality: What It Is and Why It Matters*, London: Church House Publishing, 2009.

O'Rourke, Benignus, *Finding Your Hidden Treasure: The Way of Silent Prayer*, London: Darton, Longman and Todd, 2010.

Ota, Cathy, 'The Conflict between Pedagogical Effectiveness and Spiritual Development in Catholic Schools' in Jane Erricker, Cathy Ota and Clive Erricker (eds), *Spiritual Education: Cultural, Religious and Social Differences: New Perspectives for the 21st Century*, Eastbourne, UK: Sussex Academic Press 2001.

Renn, Stephen D., *Expository Dictionary of Bible Words: Word Studies for Key English Bible Words Based on the Hebrew and Greek Texts*, Peabody, MA: Hendrickson Publishers, 2005.

Rilke, Rainer Maria, 'Buddha in Glory' in *Ahead of All Parting: The Selected Poetry and Prose of Rainer Maria Rilke*, New York: Random House, 1995.

Rohr, Richard, *Immortal Diamond: The Search for Our True Self*, London: SPCK Publishing, 2013.

Ross, Maggie, *Silence: A User's Guide* (Volume 1: Process), London: Darton, Longman and Todd Ltd, 2014.

——, *Writing the Icon of the Heart: In Silence Beholding*, Abingdon, UK: The Bible Reading Fellowship, 2011.

Russell, Bertrand, *The Problems of Philosophy*, London: Oxford University Press, 1912.

Sanai, Hakim, 'No Tongue Can Tell Your Secret', Priya Hemenway (trans.) in *The Book of Everything: Journey of the Hearts Desire*, Kansas: Andrews McMeel Publishing, 2002.

Sardello, R. and C. Sanders-Sardello, *Silence: The Mystery of Wholeness*, Berkeley, California: Goldenstone Press, 2008.

Simon, Madeleine, *Born Contemplative: Introducing Children to Christian Meditation*, London: Darton, Longman and Todd, 1993.

Saint Symeon the New Theologian, 'Hymn 1' in *The Book of Mystical Chapters: Meditations on the Soul's Ascent from the Desert Fathers and Other Early Christian Contemplatives*, Boulder, CO: Shambhala Publications, 2003.

St Augustine, *The Confessions of St Augustine*, London: Fontana, 1996.

——, 'Sermon 38 on the New Testament' in Philip Schaff (ed.), *The Early Church Fathers: Nicene and Post-Nicene Fathers, First Series*, Vol. 6, Buffalo, NY: Christian Literature Publishing Company, 1888.

Taylor, Joanne, *Inner Wisdom: Children as Spiritual Guides*, New York: Pilgrim Press, 1989.

Todres, Les, *Embodied Enquiry: Phenomenological Touchstones for Research, Psychotherapy and Spirituality*, Basingstoke, UK: Palgrave Macmillan, 2007.

Tolle, Eckhart, *Guardians of Being*, Novato, CA: New World Library, 2009.

——, *The Power of Now: A Guide to Spiritual Enlightenment*, Novato, CA: New World Library, 2010.

van Manen, Max, *Phenomonology of Practice: Meaning-Giving Methods in Phenomenological Research and Writing*, Walnut Creek, CA: Left Coast Press, Inc., 2014.

Vanier, Jean, *Signs: Seven Words of Hope*, Toronto, ON: Novalis Publishing, 2014.

Bibliography

Vatican, 'Nostrae Aetate (1965)' in Austin Flannery (ed.), *Vatican Council II: Constitutions, Decrees, Declarations: The Basic Sixteen Documents*, Dublin Dominican Publications, 1996.

Libreria Editrice Vaticana, *Catechism of the Catholic Church*, London: Burns and Oates, 1994.

Waaijman, Kees, 'Challenges of Spirituality in Contemporary Times' in *Spirituality Forum III*, University of Santo Tomas, Manila, Philippines, 2003. www.isa.org.ph/pdf/Waaijman.pdf accessed 4 December 2014

Weare, Katherine, 'Evidence for the Impact of Mindfulness on Children and Young People', 2012.

Wilber, Ken, *Integral Spirituality: A Startling New Role for Religion in the Modern and Postmodern World*, Boston: Integral Books, 2006.

Will, Andrea et al., 'Mindfulness-Based Stress Reduction for Women Diagnosed with Breast Cancer', *Cochrane Database of Systematic Reviews*, 2, 2015.

Wynne, Alexander, *The Origin of Buddhist Meditation*, New York: Routledge, 2007.